Landscapes of
MALLORCA
a countryside guide
Fourth edition

Valerie Crespí-Green

SUNFLOWER
BOOKS

Fourth edition
Revised printing 1999
Copyright © 1998, 1999
Sunflower Books™
12 Kendrick Mews
London SW7 3HG, UK

ISBN 1-85691-103-9

Centuries-old olive tree below Lluc

Important note to the reader

We have tried to ensure that the descriptions and maps in this book are
error-free at press date. The book will be updated, where necessary,
whenever future printings permit. It will be very helpful for us to receive
your comments (sent in care of the publishers, please) for the updating
of future printings.

    We also rely on those who use this book — especially walkers — to
take along a good supply of common sense when they explore.
Conditions can change fairly rapidly on Mallorca, and ***storm damage
or bulldozing may make a route unsafe at any time***. If the route is not
as we outline it here, and your way ahead is not secure, return to the
point of departure. ***Never attempt to complete a tour or walk under
hazardous conditions!*** Please read carefully the notes on pages 49 to
55, as well as the introductory comments at the beginning of each tour
and walk (regarding road conditions, equipment, grade, distances and
time, etc). Explore ***safely***, while at the same time respecting the beauty
of the countryside.

Cover photograph: landscape near the Coves de Campanet
Title page: old well at Valldemossa

Photographs: cover and pages 15, 21, 90: Brian Anderson; pages 1, 2,
    6, 18 (centre), 19, 22, 24, 27, 33, 36-7, 38, 42, 43, 44, 47, 56, 61, 62,
    63, 65 (top), 72-3, 81, 93, 96 (second from top), 98 (bottom), 102,
    104-5, 112, 113, 115, 117, 119, 122, 124 (left), 127 (top), 129 (bot-
    tom), 133: John Underwood; pages 29, 98 (top), 109, 124 (right), 127
    (bottom): Lawrence Crawley; pages 31, 96 (top), 114: Jan Taylor; page
    136: Joaquín Ranero Gascon; all other photographs by the author
Maps: John Underwood
A CIP catalogue record for this book is available from the British Library.
Printed and bound in the UK by Brightsea Press, Exeter

10 9 8 7 6 5

❀ Contents

3

❋ Preface

When you think of Mallorca, do you imagine a typical holiday island — hotels and souvenir shops strung out along busy esplanades … bars advertising 'English Fish and Chips' and 'Tea Like Mum Makes' … a multitude of night clubs and discos with large and gaudy posters promoting flamenco shows? Do you think this is Mallorca? I hope not.

Of course, the hotel-crowded esplanades *do* exist, but beyond the tourist centres, an exciting and altogether different Mallorca awaits your discovery. And with this fourth edition of *Landscapes of Mallorca,* I hope to help you to find it.

The book is divided into three main parts — **picnicking**, **touring** and **walking**, each with its own introduction. Do take a look at each introductory section, even if you think it may not apply to your holiday plans. You may find something of interest, because each section of the book has been written with one aim in view — to help you discover the 'hidden' Mallorca that most tourists never used to see … until publication of the first edition of this book in 1984. Up until then, these ancient routes across our beautiful landscapes — over the high mountains and through hidden valleys — were virtually unknown to most visitors to the island

Motorists will find that the six car tours cover more than enough territory for the average visit. The touring map has purposely been kept to a compact, easy-to-use format. It is up-to-date and contains information not found on other maps — for instance, where some roads are now closed to motorists, picnic sites with tables, and the location of walks along the route of your car tour.

Picnickers can travel by private or public transport to all the picnic spots — some of them chosen for their delightful surroundings, others for their far-reaching views. All of the picnic suggestions make excellent 'leg-stretchers' during the course of a car tour, when there's no time to fit in a longer walk.

Walkers of all ages and abilities will enjoy discovering the island's hidden landscapes, as they cross an incredible variety of terrain — some spectacular, some serene. For beginners, there are easy strolls along flat tracks (for instance, Short walk 12a, and others (like Walk 4b or Short walk 15) on delightful country lanes. Hardy walkers can tackle more challenging terrain to *miradors* only accessible on foot, and experts can scale mountain peaks or descend into the depths of the Pareis gorge …

Acknowledgements

I am extremely grateful for the invaluable help of the following:

For guiding: Mauricio Espinar, without whose knowledge and experience I could not have written the first edition of this book.

For permission to adapt their maps: The Servicio Geográfico del Ejército, Madrid.

For checking the walks and accompanying me: Clive Scott, the late George Clarke, Mary Clarke, Elizabeth and Klaus Pffeifer, Ann White, and Karen Roberts.

Poppy fields in May

Getting about

There is no doubt that a **hired car** is the most convenient way of getting about on Mallorca, and car rental on the island is good value. Be sure to 'shop around' amongst the many car-hire firms (where English is generally spoken); the prices can vary by up to perhaps 40 per cent!

The second most flexible form of transport is to hire a **taxi** and, especially if three or four people are sharing the cost, this becomes an attractive idea. If you're making a taxi journey outside the city centre (an un-metered journey), do agree on the price before setting out; all taxi-drivers should carry an official price list.

Coach tours are the most popular way of seeing the island, and convoys of tourist-loaded coaches converge onto the roads during the summer season, much to the frustration of the local drivers (and tourists in hired cars). However, you can get to know the island comfortably in this way, before embarking on your own adventures.

The most economical way of getting about is by local transport — hourly **train** services on the Palma/Inca line; the 'wild-west' **narrow-gauge railway** between Palma and Sóller; the tram between Sóller and the Port, and the local **bus** network. All these public transport systems are economical, reliable — and fun! The Sóller train is one of the island's best-known tourist attractions. But the train between Palma and Inca is also amusing: the run is a flat one across the plain, and the train hurtles along like a bullet. Remember, too, that you'll have very good views perched up on bus seats and that, generally, the buses are new and very comfortable. (Note that outside Palma you can flag down a bus anywhere along its route, without making for the centre of a village.)

The following two pages show bus and train departure points in Palma. Bus stops and taxi ranks in Sóller are indicated on the town plan on page 100. On pages 137-139 you'll find public transport timetables current at the time of writing, but *please do not rely solely on the timetables in this book;* changes to timetables are fairly frequent. Obtain a listing from the nearest tourist office as soon as you arrive on the island. Finally, do remember that local transport will be much busier on Sundays and holidays.

KEY

1 Tourist offices (three locations)
2 Town hall
3 Police
4 Post office
5 Sant Pere Bastion
6 Flea market
7 Museum (arts and crafts)
8 Mallorca Museum
9 Marqués de Palmer Palace
10 Arab baths
11 Episcopal Palace museum)
12 Cathedral
13 Sollerich Palace
14 Almundaina Palace
15 La Lonja
16 Maritime museum
17 Yacht club
18 Sta Eulalia
19 Sant Françesc
20 Market
21 Hospital

🚐 Bus departure points (a to c)
🚕 Taxi ranks
⛽ Petrol stations
🅿 Parking

Transport departure points

All trains depart from the stations facing the Plaça Espanya (🚐).
At time of writing, all buses depart from the bus station in the Plaça Espana (🚐 c), *except for* the following:
Andratx/Sant Elm: departs from stops labelled 🚐 **b** — opposite Sóller station, on Eusebi Estada; also Via Portugal and Plaça Progres
Valldemossa: departs from stop labelled 🚐 **a**: Bar la Granja, Arxiduc Lluis Salvador 1 (north of the Plaça Espanya)

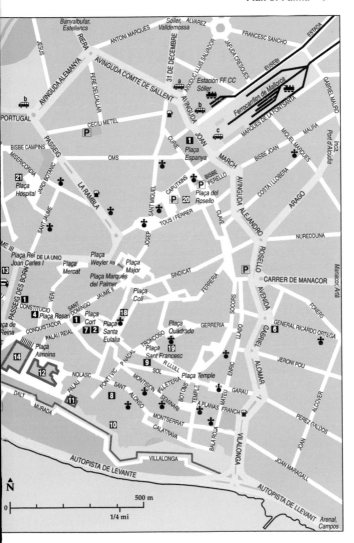

Useful addresses/telephone numbers

Tourist office, Palma (Sant Domingo 11): 724090
Tourist information kiosk, Plaça Espanya: 711527
Tourist information kiosk, airport: 260803
Train station, Plaça Espanya
    Trains to Sóller: 752051 or 752028
    Trains to Inca: 752245
Central hotel/apartment reservations: 706006
Tourist office, Sóller (Plaça de Sa Constitució): 630200
Tourist office, Port de Pollença (Carretera de Formentor 31): 865447
Tourist office, Valldemossa (Cartuja de Valldemossa): 612106

Picnicking

Picnicking can be great fun on Mallorca, provided you choose either an established picnic site created by SEFO-BASA or an open area along the course of one of the walks. Much of Mallorca's land is in private hands — although it might appear to be open countryside. So never cross fences or picnic in enclosed fields, or you might find yourselves confronted by an irate landowner!

Our Local Forestry Commission, the SErvicio FOrestal de BAleares SA (SEFOBASA) administers several areas as beauty spots for public enjoyment. These sites with tables (and often other facilities) are indicated both in the car touring notes and on the touring map by the symbol ⋔. However, if you prefer a 'get away from it all' picnic — or if you find that the established sites are too crowded (possible in the summer and on Sundays and holidays) — why not try a picnic spot along the route of one of the walks?

All the information you need to get to these 'private' picnics is given on the following pages, where *picnic numbers correspond to walk numbers,* so that you can quickly find the general location on the island by looking at the touring map (where the area of each walk is outlined in green). Under each picnic description, you'll find walking times, a map reference, and transport details (🚐, 🚌: how to get there by bus or train; 🚗: car or taxi parking). The exact location of the picnic spot is shown on the appropriate *walking map* by the symbol *P*. To help you choose an appealing setting, photographs are included for many of the picnic suggestions.

Please remember that these picnics are 'off the beaten track': wear sensible shoes and take a **sunhat** (○ alerts you to a picnic spot in full sun). It's a good idea to take along a plastic sheet as well, in case the ground is damp or prickly. **If you're travelling to your picnic by public transport**, refer to the timetables on pages 137-139, but do remember to pick up the latest timetables once you arrive on the island. **If you are travelling by car**, watch out for animals and children on the country roads, and always drive very carefully through villages. Without damaging plants, do park well off the road; *never* block a road or track.

All picnickers should read the country code on page 54 and go quietly in the countryside.

1a CALA BASSET (map page 68)

🚌 to Sant Elm; 40min on foot. Or 🚗 to Sant Elm; 25min on foot (park at Ca'n Tomeví). Use notes for Walk 1 (page 64) to walk or drive to Ca'n Tomeví and go from there down to the cove (Cala Basset).

1b TORRE DE CALA BASSET (map page 68, photographs page 65)

🚌 and 🚗 as 1a above. Use notes for Walk 1 (page 64) to walk or drive to Ca'n Tomeví, where there is room to park a few cars alongside the fence. Go left past the fenced-off area, following the sandy track. Cross a vague track a few minutes later and continue along the path, coming up onto a wide track that ascends from Sant Elm. Turn right and keep up to the top of the rise. When the track ends, go right, following a narrow earthen path through the woods (waymarked with red paint daubs). Later the path descends gently towards the ancient watchtower perched on the cliff-edge above the beach of Cala Basset. Return the same way if you parked at Ca'n Tomeví; otherwise follow the wide track all the way down to the bus stop in the square.

1c PUIG BASSET (map pages 68-69) ○

🚌 to S'Arracó (ask for the cemetery just past the village) or 🚗 (to KM5) at S'Arracó; 30min on foot. Follow the Alternative walk on page 68 but, instead of turning left at the corner of the fence, keep straight ahead up the hill along a narrow winding path. At about 20min turn left at a junction; another ten minutes will bring you up to a stone shelter. The picnic spot is at a viewpoint another minute up to the left, perched on the rocky brow of the mountain. Magnificent views towards Dragonera and over the southwest coast!

1d WINDMILLS OF S'ARRACO (map page 69) ○

🚌 or 🚗 to S'Arracó; 15min on foot. From the main street, take the Calle del Atajo (just by the side of the road to the port). At the top of this street turn left on a narrow earthen path. It winds up steeply through the trees, and in 15min comes up to the first windmill. There is a wide balcony roof (in full sun) where you can sit and enjoy your picnic, surrounded by the most wonderful panorama! For even better views, climb up inside the windmill, but take care on the unprotected stone steps. The other windmill, a few metres away to the left, is *not* safe to climb. (Unfortunately, the watchtower further up the hill commanding excellent views down over the port of Andratx is private property and cannot be visited.) You can return via the road (a few minutes down the wide track): go left for S'Arracó and the bus stop.

2 ESTELLENCS OVERLOOK (map page 71) ○

🚗 Only accessible by car; 30min on foot. See Walk 2, page 70: drive to the Font d'es Pí and then follow Walk a for 30min. Wonderful views down over Estellencs on the coast, from the flanks of Galatzó — mostly in full sun, but with a little shade on the rocky outcrop.

3 SON FORTUNY (map page 70) 🇦

🚗 Only accessible by car; 25min on foot. Drive to KM97 on the C710 and park well off the road. Follow Walk 3 (page 77) for 25min. A beautiful, peaceful picnic area in the quiet woodlands of the northern foothills below Galatzó. Tables and benches; plenty of shade.

At Santa Eugènia (Picnic 4): fields, cross monument and old wine press hidden in a cave

4a PUIG DE SANTA EUGENIA (map page 82, photographs above and page 81) ○

🚌 (only convenient on Sundays) or 🚗 to Santa Eugènia; 25min on foot. Walk up to the main square with the fountain, the Plaça de Bernardo de Santa Eugènia, and continue up the steep hill by the side of the 'Ajuntament' (town hall). Once up onto the level tarmac lane at the top, turn right and walk to the end, then go left up the stony, walled-in track. Where this ends, go through the gap in the wall, to follow a narrow earthen path up to the top of the hill. Go over the low wall by the side of an old pine, and on up to the cross monument. Excellent vistas from this point — almost the entire island is visible! No shade. Can be very windy in winter.

4b SO NA ROSSA (map page 83) ○

🚌 (only convenient on Sundays) or 🚗 to Santa Eugènia (drive to the end of the village, towards Algaida, and park in the lane on the right, by the orchard wall — as described in Walk b on page 82); 55min on foot. Follow Walk b on page 82 for 50min, then turn down left. Some minutes further down, a grassy lane goes off left, bordered by a low stone wall. You can sit here and enjoy your picnic, with a magnificent view across the plain to the distant mountains. No shade.

5a FONT D'ES POLLS (map page 86) 🍴

🚌 or 🚗 to Valldemossa; 50min on foot. Follow Short walk 2 (page 84) as far as the picnic site, by an old well. Wooden tables and benches. Plenty of shade from the poplars, but no views.

5b VALLDEMOSSA OVERLOOK (map page 86, photograph of Valldemossa page 22)

🚌 or 🚗 to Valldemossa; 1h20min on foot. This is a very long walk for a picnic, but I wanted to include this in the picnic section because of its spectacular position! Follow Alternative walk 5 (page 84) as far as the viewpoint — *not* the first rocky outcrop after the bend, but the *second* one, a little further along, where a narrow stone-edged path (marked by a small red arrow at ground level) leads off right to a natural 'platform'. Stunning panoramic views over Valldemossa and the surrounding mountains, down as far as the coast. Sun or shade.

6a SA FORADADA OVERLOOK (map page 86, photograph page 24)

🚐 or 🚗 to Son Marroig; 5min on foot. This setting is near Walk 6, but *not* on the route of the walk. See Car tour 2, page 23: from the house of Son Marroig, go over the stile and walk down the wide track towards the sea to this picnic area — stone seats around a natural rocky 'platform'. Sun or shade, with views down over the famous 'pierced rock' (Sa Foradada) jutting out into the sea.

6b FONT DE SON COLL (map page 86) ○

🚐 or 🚗 to Deià; 40min on foot. Follow Short walk 2 (page 89) to the stone steps just beyond the hamlet of Son Coll, and turn left down to the mountain spring, where you can picnic on a stone seat by the small pool. Little shade; no far-reaching views.

7 ORIENT VALLEY (map page 94, photographs pages 96, 98) ○

🚗 Only accessible by car; 30min on foot. Park at KM11.9 on the Alaró/Orient road, or nearby, well off the road. Follow Walk 7 (page 93) for 30min, to picnic on the small grassy outcrop. Panoramic views down over the peaceful Orient valley. Mostly in sun, but there is a shady clearing a little further up.

9 ES BARRANC (map on reverse of touring map, photo page 101)

🚗 to Biniaraix; 10-15min on foot. Or 🚐 or 🚌 to Sóller; 45min on foot (but consider taking a taxi to from Sóller to Biniaraix, then you will only have to walk 15min). Follow Walk 9 on page 99 as far as the 45min-point — or further; choose a picnic spot anywhere along Es Barranc. There are plenty of lovely rocks pools and bridges to choose from, in sun or in shade.

10 SA FONT DE BALITX (map on reverse of touring map, nearby photograph page 102)

🚐 *(restricted timetable)* or 🚗 to the Mirador de Ses Barques; 35min on foot. Follow Walk 10 (page 102) for 35min, to picnic by the mountain spring or on the grassy terrace nearby. Sun or shade. Lovely valley views on the way.

11 SA CALOBRA (map on reverse of touring map, photograph pages 104-105) ○

🚗, 🚐 or ⚓ to Sa Calobra; 15-20min on foot. Walk through the tunnels (take care; the surface underfoot is uneven) to the shingle beach, and explore as far as you like up the Pareis Gorge; there are many good picnic spots, but little shade. Do not attempt to venture beyond the first large boulders without adequate climbing equipment.

12 CUBER LAKE (map on reverse of touring map, overview photograph page 109) ○

🚐 *(restricted timetable)* or 🚗 to the Cúber Lake; 10-30min on foot. Leave your transport at the small parking area at KM34 on the C710, by the Cúber Lake. Go through the access gate; there are plenty of grassy picnic spots off the track only a few minutes downhill, with expansive views across the lake to the surrounding mountain peaks.

There is also a SEFOBASA stone refuge with a picnic table and bench at the far end of the lake (30min on foot), which may be used if no one is staying at the refuge. This is a spectacular spot, with impressive views of the lake and the Puig Major. The area is also a bird-watchers' paradise. No shade.

13a GORG BLAU OVERLOOK (map on reverse of touring map, photograph page 112) ○

🚌 (restricted timetable) or 🚗 to the Cúber Lake (park as for Picnic 12); 15-30min on foot. Follow *Walk 12* (page 109), taking the maintenance path alongside the watercourse as far as you like. There are several good picnic spots along the way, on rocky outcrops, with superb views down over the Gorg Blau lake hidden between the island's two highest mountains — Massanella and the Puig Major. Little shade.

13b FONT D'ES PRAT DE MASSANELLA (map on reverse of touring map, photographs pages 61, 112, 113)

🚌 (restricted timetable) or 🚗 to the Cúber Lake; 1h on foot. Follow *Walk 12* (page 109), taking the maintenance path alongside the watercourse, but continue over the bridge, following the text as far as the 55min-point. Then pick up notes for Walk 13, page 112, to go to the Font d'es Prat. Picnic in the shady clearing by the spring. No far-reaching views at the picnic spot, but plenty along the way!

15a LLUC VALLEY OVERLOOK (map on reverse of touring map)

🚌 or 🚗 to Lluc monastery; 15-20min on foot. Go to the left of the monastery building, and walk up the wide steps; a shady trail leads up to the top of the hill by the cross monument. Plenty of sunny or shady spots for picnicking, with excellent views over the valley and the monastery.

15b LLUC (map on reverse of touring map) 🎌

🚌 or 🚗 to Lluc monastery; 5-20min on foot. There are many lovely picnic areas in and around Lluc, with sun, shade, and drinking fountains; there's a good picnic spot directly in front of the car park at Lluc itself. But why not follow Walk 15 (page 118) and picnic somewhere along the picturesque old track, or by the camping site where you can use the barbecues? It's only about 20min along.

15c BINIBONA (map page 120)

🚌 to Caimari; 40min on foot, or 🚗 to Binibona; 15-20min on foot. Walk or drive along the quiet country lane from Caimari to the wide square in Binibona (park well tucked in). Then follow the track off right at the far end of the square into the woods for as long as you like. About fifteen minutes along here, you can cross the streambed down to the right, to find a good picnic spot.

16 BINIFALDO (map on reverse of touring map, photograph page 122)

🚌 or 🚗 to Lluc monastery; 30-50min on foot. Follow *Walk 15* (page 118), and turn into the old route towards Binifaldó. Follow it as far as you like; there are many good picnic spots along the way, where

*The author at Penya Rotja
(Picnic 20b)*

weathered limestone rocks form natural 'tables', in sun or in shade. (*Note:* If you are travelling by car, the gates to the Binifaldó water-bottling plant are open Mondays to Fridays, saving you 20-25min walking. Turn in at the KM17.4 marker on the C710 and park by the gates at Menut, well off the side of the lane, or go through the gates and park less than 2km along, below the big house of Binifaldó at the foot of Tomir.)

17 SEFOBASA PICNIC SITES (map on reverse of touring map) ⴲ

🚌 *(restricted timetable)* or 🚐 to KM16.5 on the C710; up to 15min on foot. You have two options: either park inside the picnic grounds and use the facilites (barbecues, running water, WCs, swing park, etc), or continue down the road for 100m/yds to KM16.4. Here you can walk through the wooden gate and follow a wide track through the woods for about 15min. You will come to a small spring (on a bend to the left), and a more secluded stone refuge higher up. There are also a couple of picnic sites on the opposite side of the road, one at KM16.4 and another further along at KM17.4. *Note:* SEFOBASA picnic sites are only crowded on local fiesta days or at weekends. All sites offer sun and shade.

18 MORTITX OVERLOOK (map page 126, nearby photograph page 127) ○

🚌 *(restricted timetable)* or 🚐 to Mortitx; 35min on foot. Leave your transport at the Mortitx gates, and follow Alternative walk 18 on page 125, to picnic on the bridge that divides a quiet creek from the cascading waters that fall into the Torrent de Mortitx. Full sun, but plenty of shady spots along the way — under some of the biggest olive trees you have ever seen. Spectacular views down over the Mortitx area. *Note:* this a SEFOBASA protected area; *walkers should only go in small groups, quietly, and keep to the track.*

19 BOQUER VALLEY (map page 129, photographs pages 128-129)

🚌 to Port de Pollença; 35-45min on foot, or 🚐 to the Oro Playa apartments at Port de Pollença on the PM221 to Formentor (park opposite the tree-lined avenue up to the Bóquer farm); 20-30min on foot. Follow Walk 19 on page 128, to head up into the Bóquer valley, and either picnic at the 'wild west ambush scene' amongst the fallen rocks and boulders for shade, or further along the route in the open valley, in full sun. Beautiful views on all sides.

20a LA VICTORIA VIEWPOINT (map page 131) ○

🚗 to the Ermita de la Victoria; 3min on foot. (You can also take a 🚌 to Alcúdia and then a taxi to the Ermita de la Victoria; remember to arrange a return pick-up time with the taxi driver.) From the car park by the old church at the *ermita,* go left down a few steps and then straight ahead, following a narrow path through the trees. It leads in a couple of minutes to a magnificent viewpoint protected by a wooden fence and complete with stone seating, overlooking the Bay of Pollença and the distant mountains of the Formentor Peninsula. Full sun.

20b PENYA ROTJA (map page 131, photograph page 15) ○

🚗 or 🚌 as 20a above; 30min on foot. Follow Walk 20 on page 131, taking the path to the Penya Rotja. You will find several picnic spots along the way, with fine views down over the Bay of Pollença and across to the Formentor Peninsula, mostly in full sun.

20c VICTORIA PARK (map page 131, photograph below) 🎪

🚗 Only accessible by car; 5min on foot. Drive from Alcúdia towards Mal Pas, and turn right by the Bodega del Sol bar, to follow the tarmac lane into the Victoria Park. Keep along for some time, and park at the wide parking area just after some steep bends. A five minute walk will bring you to the picnic site at a pass at the end of the road, the Coll Baix. Here there is plenty of shade, a stone refuge, tables and benches, and a drinking fountain. Or you can walk down to Coll Baix Beach to picnic (35min on foot): descend the wide path from the picnic site — you will have to scramble over large boulders at the end (not ideal if you are carrying a heavy picnic bag).

21 CALA MALSOC (map page 134, nearby photograph page 133)

🚗 Only accessible by car; 30min on foot. See page 133: 'How to get there' and drive to Cala Estreta to park. Then follow Walk 21 as far as Cala Malsoc, to picnic in sun or shade, in this lovely sandy cove bordered by pine woods. Beautiful sea views.

22 CALA BELTRÁN (map page 135)

🚌 or 🚗 to Cala Pí; 25min on foot. Follow Walk 22 (page 135) to Cala Beltrán. There's ample sun, shade and privacy in this sheltered little cove.

Idyllic Coll Baix Beach, below the setting for Picnic 20c

1 SPECTACULAR SOUTHWEST SETTINGS

Palma • Peguera • Port d'Andratx • Andratx • Sant Elm • Estellencs • Banyalbufar • La Granja • Puigpunyent • La Reserva de Galatzó • Palma

120km/74mi; 4h driving

On route: ⊼ at the Galatzó Nature Reserve; Picnics (see pages 10-16): 1a, 1b, 1c, 1d, (2), 3; Walks: 1, (2a), 2b, 2c, 3

A leisurely, all-day tour with plenty of interesting places to stop off Remember to allow a couple of hours' daylight at the end to enjoy the Galatzó Nature Reserve. The roads are good, but narrow and winding between Andratx and Banyalbufar.

Opening hours/market days
La Granja is open daily from 10.00-18.00; exhibition of Mallorcan folk dancing in typical costume Wednesdays and Fridays at 15.30 and 17.00.
La Reserva de Galatzó (Tel: 616622) is open daily from 10.00-18.00 in winter (tickets can be purchased up to 16.00) and 10.00-20.00 in summer (tickets can be purchased up to 18.00).
Market in Andratx: Wednesday mornings

Leave Palma by driving west along the beautiful, palm-shaded Paseo Marítimo, passing the Club de Mar, where many expensive yachts moor, and the commercial port and naval zone of Porto Pí. The motorway continues ahead (signposted to Andratx) and climbs gradually above the resort of Cala Mayor, hidden by high-rise apartment blocks. Soon, the Castell de Bendinat★ (8km ▮) appears on the left — a beautiful neo-Gothic palace surrounded by parklands, now privately owned and closed to the public; below it is the Bendinat Golf Club. Further along we pass by the resorts of Illetes, Portals Nous with its Marineland aquarium, and Palma Nova; then the motorway ends and becomes the C719. Continue past turn-offs to Mallorca's casino, Magalluf and Santa Ponça (⛽ 15km).

Soon we come to Peguera (21km), but continue along the main road through two tunnels (Peguera's promenade has now been pedestrianised, and it is better to enter at the far end to avoid a confusing drive through the back streets). Turn off left at 24km (signposted 'Camp de Mar') and drive downhill, keeping left for **Peguera** (🔺✕🍴⊕), where you can park and explore on foot.

Return to Camp de Mar and

Port d'Andratx
19

follow the signposts to drive over the pine-covered hill and down into scenic **Port d'Andratx** (31km ▲▲✕🍷); there are two municipal car parks which make for easy parking, so you can wander through the narrow streets at leisure, or take some refreshment at one of the port-side cafés. Or you can drive up onto Sa Mola (signposted) to admire the views across to the Isle of Dragonera which we'll see later today.

Leaving this picturesque harbour scene behind you, take the wide road out of the port, driving between almond orchards and farmhouses, to come into the town of **Andratx** (Spanish: Andraitx; 35km ⚷▲▲✕🍷⊕). Keeping along to the junction, turn left into the centre. Some 400m along you'll find the beginning of the C710, signposted to Estellencs (Walk 1 ends here). We follow this road later in the tour, but for now keep ahead — you will come onto the PM103. Turn left to follow this very pretty country lane, meandering over the hills. We pass through **S'Arracó** (39km *P*1c, 1d), where two alternative versions of Walk 1 begin and end, and come into **Sant Elm** (Spanish: San Telmo; 42km ▲▲✕*P*1a, 1b) — a quiet fishing village in winter, a peaceful resort in summer. Here you can stretch your legs by visiting the watchtower shown on page 65 (use the notes for Picnic 1b) … or you can simply drive to the end of the road for a good view of the Isle of Dragonera across the stretch of blue water. Walk 1 begins here, and its shorter version, ideal for motorists, ends here.

Back in Andratx, follow signs for Palma, and turn left where you see the sign 'Centro Villa'. Turn right on the main street, then take the next left (C710). Now we wind up through a green landscape of pine-clad hills and mountains, towards the rugged western coastline of steep cliffs and rocky inlets. At the **Mirador de Ses Ortigues** (60km 📷) the pines have grown so tall that it is hardly possible to glimpse the view of the the the little *cala* below. The road winds down and through two tunnels, and soon we come to the cliff-top restaurant of Es Grau (64km ✕) and the adjoining **Mirador de Ricardo Roca★** (📷). The stone steps lead up to a precarious viewpoint and stone shelter (a good place to picnic), with splendid panoramic views along this wild stretch of coastline.

The C710 now dives down through the small tunnel of Es Grau and hugs the coast. At the KM97 marker you pass a stony track on the right: it leads to a magnificent picnic area with barbecues up in the woods (*P*3) and is also the starting point for Walks 2c and 3. At the **Coll d'es Pí** (71km ✕🍷📷) the road turns inland and down into **Estellencs**

(72km ♣▲✕⊕). This delightful mountain village sits at the foot of Mount Galatzó, setting for Walk 2. The fertile, terraced slopes, irrigated by channelled mountain springs, are studded with orange groves and olive trees. The road narrows somewhat as it leaves the village and snakes its way to the **Talaia de Ses Animes**★ (74km 📷; photograph below and page 61), a renovated watchtower where you can park and cross the bridge for more magnificent coastal views, especially of the sloping cultivated terraces shown below. Next we come to **Banyalbufar** (76km ▲✕⊕), set on slopes above the sea. It's worth turning down sharp left in front of the Hotel Mar i Vent and following the narrow streets downhill; there's a parking area further down, and one can visit a quaint little cemetery overlooking the sea.

From here the road swings inland once more, undulating over the hills through thick pine forests. At the next junction, keep straight on for Esporles along the PM110,

The terraces of Banyalbufar from the Talaia de Ses Animes

and then turn right onto the PMV110-1 (85km; signposted to Puigpunyent). On the left here is the entrance to **La Granja★**. This large, splendid mansion once belonged to the Cistercian monks and later to an aristocratic Mallorcan family, but the archways and ornamental fountains evoke its Moorish past. It is certainly worth a visit.

From La Granja continue along the narrow and twisting road towards Puigpunyent, climbing over the hills and through pretty valleys and passing Sa Campaneta (95km), another mansion converted into a rural hotel. Come into the pretty mountain village of **Puigpunyent** (99km; Walk 2b) and drive down to a junction. Keep straight ahead through the village, but about 200m further uphill, turn right for 'La Reserva'. The road soon starts to climb. At the three-way junction, keep to the middle fork. (To the right is the road to the Font d'es Pí; **P**2 and Walk 2a.) This is the entrance to the Galatzó Nature Reserve, **La Reserva★** (101km ⌱). With its waterfalls and bridges, luxuriant vegetation and mountain scenery, it's a nature-lover's paradise.

Back in Puigpunyent, turn right at the junction for Palma. Enter the city (120km) by keeping ahead at both roundabouts, or go left or right at second roundabout onto the ring road, to find your relevant exit.

The bell tower of the monastery rises above Valldemossa (Car tour 2). Originally the site of a Moorish palace, the buildings were later the retreat of King Sancho. After his death, the place was given to the Carthusian monks who, little by little, constructed the monastery. When this religious order was expelled from Spain in 1835, private owners took over and rented the cells to travellers — including the poet Ruben Darío and the writers Unamuno and Azorín.

2 PRETTY MOUNTAIN VILLAGES

Palma • Valldemossa • Port de Valldemossa • Ermita de Sa Trinitat • Son Marroig • Deià • Port de Sóller • Balearic Museum of Natural Science (Sóller) • Gardens of Alfabia • Palma

90km/56mi; 4h driving

On route: ☗ at the Ermita de Sa Trinitat and Son Marroig; Picnics (see pages 10-16): 5a, 5b, 6a, 6b; Walks: 5, 6

I suggest you make a full day of this short tour, as there are so many interesting places to visit along the way. The roads are mostly good, although mountainous. The road down to Port Valldemossa is narrow and winding in places.

Opening hours/market days
The **Carthusian Monastery** (Valldemossa) is open daily except Sundays, Christmas Day and New Year's Day, from 09.30-13.00 and 15.00-17.30 in winter and from 09.30-13.00 and 15.00-18.30 in summer (the museums close 30 minutes later). Live piano concerts (Chopin) hourly every day (except Mondays and Thursday mornings, when there are folk dancing exhibitions) from 10.30 until 13.20.
Son Marroig (Deià) is open daily (except Sundays) from 10.00-18.30, but sometimes closes a little earlier on dark winter evenings.
The **Balearic Museum of Natural Science and Botanical Gardens** (Sóller) are open daily (except Mondays) from 10.00-14.00 and 15.30-17.00 (October-March), 10.30-13.30 and 17.00- 20.00 (April-September). On Sundays and public holidays from 10.30-13.30 only.
The **Gardens of Alfabia** are open daily (except Sundays) from 09.30 17.30; open Saturday mornings only, from 09.30-13.00.
Market in Sóller: Saturday mornings

From Palma's ring road (Vía Cintura) take the exit to Valldemossa, joining the PM111 (☗) which takes you through almond orchards and farmlands towards the low, pine-covered hills below the sierra. The glass-blowing factory just past **S'Esgleieta** (8.5km) makes an interesting stop-off if you set out early enough. Soon the road starts to climb gradually between slopes clad with olive trees towards the picturesque mountain village where Chopin and George Sand spent the winter of 1838-9; the blue-tiled bell tower of the monastery where they rented cells is clearly visible from the road as we wind up towards the mountains.

Come into **Valldemossa**★ (17km ☗☗✕⊕M*P*5a, 5b), and park at any of the car parks on the right of the main road, opposite the colourful road-side cafés. Then cross and follow the cobbled streets up to the square and monastery (see opposite). A ticket to the monastery includes a visit to Chopin's quarters (containing one of his pianos, his death mask, and some original manuscripts, letters and documents), a very interesting 17th-century pharmacy, various exhibits (including one of Europe's oldest printing presses), art collections, and the palace of King Sancho.

23

Son Marroig: the marble dome in the gardens was made for the Archduke Luis Salvador in Italy — a poetic reminder of a romantic past.

There are also Mallorcan folk dancing performances in traditional dress and piano recitals (Chopin of course) by brilliant young pianists most mornings. Nearby tourist shops sell carved olive-wood objects and hand-embroidered shawls. Walk 5 begins and ends here.

Leave the village in direction of Andratx/Sóller (signposted). You will see the large old house of Son Moragues with its stone arches up to the right just outside Valldemossa; this was one of the Archduke Luis Salvador of Austria's many mansions. Pass the turn-off right to Deià (19km; C710), and turn left down the little road down to Valldemossa's Port (PMV1131) some 300m further along. *Please drive carefully* down this narrow, tortuous road cut into the cliff. **Port de Valldemossa** (24km ✕), surrounded by high red cliffs, is a quaint little fishing hamlet sitting on the rocks — now edged by one or two more modern dwellings. Return to the C710 and keep left towards Deià (☎ at 29km). Not very far along, look out for the narrow turning up right signposted 'Ermita' (just before the entrance to the restaurant Ca'n Costa. The way up to the **Ermita de Sa Trinitat** (30km 🛉🏓📷) is only wide enough for one car, but there are several 'passing places' and plenty of room to park and turn around at the top. (If you don't fancy driving up, park by Ca'n Costa and walk up.) Visit the tiny chapel and the small interior patio — from where you can enjoy a superb coastal view. There is also a delightful picnic area under the trees.

Again rejoining the C710, continue past Miramar — another early acquisition of the Archduke Luis Salvador. It's not long before we come to **Son Marroig★** (37km ✕📷M), the archduke's principal residence. Here we find good parking, *miradors* from which to view the famous rock Sa Foradada, pierced with a hole … and a fine picnic spot just below the house (**P**6a). After viewing the marble dome in the gardens, go into the house; a tour of the rooms containing the original furniture, several of his excellent sketches and paintings, writings, portraits and photographs of his family, amply repays the small entrance fee. Luis

Salvador's exceptional love for Mallorca's natural history is very much in evidence. One can also walk down to Sa Foradada; it takes just under an hour, but you must ask permission at the house first.

Continue along the coast to the incredibly picturesque mountain village of **Deià★** (40km ✝🔺✕M*P*6b; photograph page 90), home of many well-known artists and poets — Robert Graves being one of the earliest to settle here. Visit, perhaps, the small but interesting archeological museum and the little church on the hilltop with a charming cemetery, where you can find Robert Graves' tombstone. Walk 6 begins at Deià.

At the village exit we pass La Residencia, Richard Branson's fine luxury hotel, and about 1km out of Deià a little road leads off left down to the shingle beach at Cala de Deià (Short walk 6-1). At KM60.2 we pass the starting point for Short walk 6-2, then the road contours above Lluc-Alcari (43km🔺✕), another artists colony you might like to visit (✕ at 46km).

More splendid views unfold: the distant high peaks of the Puig Major and lower mountains surrounding the Sóller basin, where a myriad of citrus and olive groves populate the pine-clad slopes. On coming to the main road (C711) in the valley, turn left and head for **Port de Sóller** (54km 🔺✕). Here amidst sun-seekers, seaside restaurants and crowded beaches, the summer comes into its own. On the other hand, it's rather desolate in winter.

Returning along the C711 (⛽ at 59km), just past the petrol station you'll find the **Balearic Museum of Natural Science** (M with **Botanical Gardens**) on the left, with plenty of parking space — quite an interesting place. Our homeward route now snakes uphill in interminable bends towards the mountain pass.* A superb view down over the Sóller valley can be seen at the *mirador*★ (📷) almost at the top, and on the south side of the **Coll de Sóller** (66km) we soon come to another viewpoint by a mountain-top café (67km ✕📷), this time overlooking Palma's bay.

Winding down the mountainside through endless olive terracing, it is not long before we can stretch our legs again at the **Gardens of Alfabia★** (a left turn at the tunnel exit; 73km ❀✕), while we explore the exotic pavilions, romantic arbours and bamboo-shaded lily ponds. The final stretch (⛽ at 88km) returns us to Palma after 90km.

*You can avoid this tortuous mountain route by going through the Sóller tunnel (toll levied) — but it would be a pity to miss the views!

3 THE MAGNIFICENT MOUNTAIN ROUTE, AND THE CAPES

Palma • Sóller • Biniaraix • Mirador de Ses Barques • Cúber and Gorg Blau lakes • Sa Calobra • Lluc • Pollença • Port de Pollença • Cap de Formentor • Alcúdia • Cap d'es Pinar • Port d'Alcúdia • Coves de Campanet • Palma

240km/149mi; 8h driving (a two-day tour)

On route: ╤ at the Mirador de Ses Barques, Sa Bassa, Cúber Lake, Lluc, C710 at km16.4, Ermita de la Victoria; Picnics (see pages 10-16): (7, 8), 9-12, 13a, 13b, 15a, 15b, (15c), 16-20; Walks: 6, (7, 8), 9-11, 12a, 12b, 13-20

This beautiful two-day tour (with a night spent at Lluc monastery set in the heart of the sierra) will take you through some of the most spectacular mountain scenery on the island, and it is generally the most popular touristic route. Therefore the roads are in good condition, although you may be slowed down by traffic in summer, and you can expect to meet tourist coaches. There are many hairpin bends on the road to Sa Calobra, although it is well surfaced.

Opening hours/market days

Lluc Monastery (for overnight stay tel: 517025) is best booked in advance in summer; otherwise just book at the information office on arrival; the monastery is open daily, but doors close at 23.00. The monastery's museum is open from 10.00-18.30 (April to September) and 10.00-17.30 (Oct to March).

Ca S'Amitger (Lluc) is open from 09.30-13.30 and 15.00-17.30.

The **Campanet Caves** are open daily from 10.00-18.00.

Markets — Sóller: Saturday mornings; **Pollença:** Sunday mornings; **Port de Pollença:** Wednesday mornings; **Alcúdia:** Tuesday and Sunday mornings

L eave Palma's ring road (Vía Cintura) at the 'Sóller' exit, to join the C711. The road heads straight as an arrow across the plain through dazzling pink and white almond orchards (in February) towards the sierra (✕ at 15km). Pass the entrance to the **Gardens of Alfabia★** (17km; Car tour 2), and then begin to climb the olive-terraced slopes as the road winds up in earnest towards the pass. (You *could* drive through the toll-paid tunnel), but you would miss out on the wonderful panoramas.) Come to the **Coll de Sóller★** (23km ✕⊡), from where there are splendid views down south over Palma's bay. Then, descending to the north, we soon come to another *mirador★* (⊡) offering a magnificent outlook over the Sóller valley surrounded by the island's highest mountains. Continue carefully down the many hairpin bends.

At the bottom of the road, take the first right turn, into **Sóller★** (33km ✝▲▲✕☐⊕M; Walks 6 and 9; plan page 100). This enchanting village is a popular tourist destination, not only because of its setting, but also because it's such fun to travel here on the narrow-gauge railway from

Sóller church

Palma through the mountain and down from amazing heights. Keep straight down this narrow road and into the centre. Biniaraix and Fornalutx are signposted here, but you might first like go left just at the tramlines, to visit the Plaça de Sa Constitució (Constitution Square), where you can enjoy refreshments beneath the colourful awnings of one of the cafés, or simply admire the beautiful façade of the 16th-century church shown above.

Now follow the Biniaraix signposts, and cross the bridge over the stream. The narrow lane leads up past the charming little square in **Biniaraix** (34.5km ♨) and round to the right. If you can squeeze into a parking space somewhere, you might like to explore the beginning of Walk 9 — a beautiful, stone-laid pilgrims' trail; it starts just opposite the road to Fornalutx, and you could follow it for five minutes (to the first little bridge; *P*9), for a lovely view of Sóller. Continuing, we follow the very narrow road towards Fornalutx, through abundant orange groves. On joining the wider PMV212-1, turn up right to **Fornalutx** (36km ♨✕⊕), one of the most picturesque villages on Mallorca. Just after passing the square (now pedestrianised) keep right to find the car park, then explore the lovely old stone-stepped streets, where open doorways show beautiful Mallorcan interiors.

Back in the car and continuing uphill, the last bar-café (opposite a car park) boasts a magnificent view down over the village and the impressive mountains that surround it. On the elevated terrace here, you can also sample one of the best *pa'amb oli*s on the island, a typical Mallorcan breakfast of local bread with olive oil, tomatoes, peppers, cured ham and green olives — very nutritious!

Leave Fornalutx now along the PM212, climbing up above the village through more orange groves and olive orchards. When you meet the C710, turn up right. Not long after, you come to the fabulous **Mirador de Ses Barques**★ (40km ✕⇌☕*P*10), with astounding views down over the bay and Port of Sóller. Walk 10 starts here. Leaving this

27

Mirador de Ses Barques

viewpoint, we continue climbing towards the peaks, with the enormous red rock mountain, the Penya d'es Migdía, looming up ahead (⋔ at Sa Bassa; 44km). Pass another *mirador* at the entrance to the first tunnel under the mountain, at the **Coll d'es Puig Major** (48km 📷). Say goodbye to this landscape now, or take a last photograph, as you'll find the scenery completely different on the other side.

Passing a small reservoir, we wind down through the military zone of Son Torrella, and then descend a tranquil, uninhabited landscape of green valleys surrounded by rocky mountains towards a first reservoir, the **Cúber Lake** (52km 📷*P*12, 13a, 13b). Many wonderful mountain hikes start here — including Alternative walk 9, Walks 12a and 12b, and Walk 13. There is also a good view from here of the radar globes atop the magnificent rocky peak of the Puig Major (1445m/4740ft), the island's highest mountain. Some 2km further along, rounding the south side of the Puig Major, we come to the **Gorg Blau** lake (54km 📷), a second, deeper reservoir, peaceful and still, where trout fishing is allowed (with permission from SEFOBASA). Then we leave this enchanting valley through another tunnel.

Shortly we reach the turn-off to Sa Calobra (PM214-1) at 57km (✖), by the huge archways of a Romanesque aqueduct. The road winds up over the bare lower slopes of the Puig Major, and then loops under itself to descend a wild and rocky wilderness in a 'thousand' bends, coming to **Sa Calobra★** (68km ▲▲ ✖), where Walks 10 and 11 end. Here some of the most stunning and grandiose scenery can be contemplated at the **Torrent de Pareis★** (the 'Twin Streams') — where, after heavy rains, the double torrent cascading down from the mountains between vertical cliffs almost 200m/650ft high reaches the sea at a small shingle

The incredible gash of the Pareis Gorge, from the C710 viewpoint

beach. To visit this setting, shown on pages 104-105, walk through the two tunnels cut in the rock (take care on the uneven surface underfoot). Boat trips run daily in summer (and on calm winter days), and this is decidedly the best way to see Mallorca's abrupt northern coastline.

Return to the C710 and turn left towards Lluc. Soon we can stop at a viewpoint★ (84km ⌕ for the stunning 'aerial' view of the Pareis Gorge shown above. Further along, by the 13th-century chapel of Sant Pere (85km ✝✗; photograph page 56) at **Escorca**, the long and tortuous footpath down into the gorge (Walk 11) begins. Keeping ahead, we eventually come to the turn-off left to Lluc at the **Coll de Sa Bataia** (90km ✗🖭; Walks 13 and 14). Should you wish to shorten the tour to just one day, keep straight on down the PM213 (**P**15c) to Inca, and return from there to Palma. But if you are game for a night at the mountain monastery and another exciting tour tomorrow, turn down left and, at the next junction, turn left to the **Santuari de Lluc**★ (92km ✝▲ ✗🅰M**P**15a, 15b; photograph page 117). The monastery is steeped in legend and history, originating in the 8th century, when a small chapel was built. The present buildings date from the 17th and 18th centuries. The church, built between 1622 and 1724, was considerably altered at the beginning of the 1900s. It is an important Catholic sanctuary; visitors come here from all over the island, and pilgrimages are often made on foot up to the monastery. The museum contains coin collections, typical dress, and items of archaeological merit. Also of great interest is the Ca S'Amitger, just by the entrance to the car park, with its colourful, illuminated photographs of Mallorca's flora and fauna, including many varieties of indigenous orchids. Here you will get an insight into the life of the great black vulture — the island, and Europe's, largest bird of prey. Of most importance to countryside lovers, however, is the opportunity to stay overnight at Lluc — the best base for many superb mountain hikes (Walks 13 and 15-17 among them). So, there's plenty to keep you busy here, until supper at one of the three local restaurants and a peaceful night's sleep in the heart of the mountains!

Day two: After breakfast at the monastery, rejoin the C710 in direction of Pollença. Pass the entrance to Binifaldó (95km *P*16; photograph page 122) — Walks 15 and 16 come this way — and then some excellent woodland picnic sites (96km ⊞*P*17). Walk 17 begins here, following the old route to Pollença. Our narrow road snakes through a dramatic rocky landscape of high mountains and valleys, passing the entrance to Mortitx at KM10.9 (*P*18; Walk 18). It then winds down toward the northern tip of the island, with magnificent views over Pollença's bay.

Come into **Pollença★** (112km ☗▲▲✕₽⊕M); just by the first turning into this market-garden town, a Roman bridge★ (⩩) — the only original one left on Mallorca, still stands over the Torrent de Sant Jordi. Behind the main square the cypress-bordered stone stairway shown on page 124 leads up to a tiny 18th-century chapel atop Calvary Hill★, from where an impressive view of the bay can be enjoyed; there are 365 steps up, one for each day of the year — a good leg-stretcher! Opposite the town one can see the Puig de Maria★ (333m/1090ft); a 45min walk to the top would take you to a hermitage with more stunning panoramic views of both Pollença and Alcúdia's bays.

Leaving Pollença we continue towards the sea along the PM220, passing the turn-off to Cala Sant Vicenç (▲▲✕) at 114km and coming into **Port de Pollença★** (118km ▲▲✕ ₽⊕M), a touristic but tranquil resort on the edge of the bay. Turning left just before the sea-front, onto the PM221 (signposted to Formentor), will make it easier to find a parking space somewhere up a side street, as no doubt you will want to explore. Walk along the beautiful traffic-free esplanade, where a multitude of bright sun umbrellas shade the sea-front cafés, and white yachts bob up and down on a deep blue sea at the marina. Or follow Walk 19 up into the Boquer valley (*P*19), a bird-watchers' paradise with panoramic views down over the port.

To continue, we keep along the PM221 towards Formentor and start to wind up several sharp bends, soon arriving at the splendidly-engineered **Mirador d'es Colomer★** (124km ▣), where stone steps skirt the edge of a high rock cliff and end at a precipitous viewpoint hundreds of feet above the sea — definitely the best place to photograph the Formentor headland and Es Colomer ('Pigeon Rock'). Opposite this viewpoint, a rough road climbs to a 16th-century watchtower, the Atalaia de Albercutx, with unsurpassed views of the Formentor and Pollença bays, but I recommend you walk up, not drive, as there is very little room to turn around at the top.

Our route continues over the pass, and winds down between pine woods towards the magnificent bay, where pale turquoise and aquamarine waters lap onto white sands. Ahead lies the famous Hotel Formentor above a private beach. Its opening in 1926 was heralded by illuminated advertisements on the Eiffel Tower, hence it became — and still is — a favourite paradise by the sea for the 'jet-set', politicians, and film stars. Continuing left, a winding road over the rocky headland (with two more *miradors*) will bring us to the northenmost tip, the **Cap de Formentor**★ (138km) and its lighthouse, perched high on the jagged cliff-tops — the home of Eleonora's falcons.

Leaving the unique beauty of the Formentor cape, we return to Port de Pollença and continue straight on around the bay. Then, going left at the roundabout, we come into **Alcúdia**★ (166km ⚑✕ and **M** of Roman antiquities), the capital city of Mallorca during Roman times. Originally named 'Pollentia', the thriving city flourished from the 2nd century BC until the 6th century, when it was destroyed by invading Vandals. Parts of the old city wall still remain, rebuilt during the reign of Jaime II, by which time the town had been renamed Alcúdia (derived from a Moorish word for 'hill'). The Roman amphitheatre is worth a visit.

At the second set of traffic lights, continue ahead, following signposts to Mal Pas, to drive along the headland towards the Cape of Pines. At the junction by the Bodega del Sol bar in **Mal Pas**, a road left leads to two beautiful sandy beaches that most tourists miss and, off to the right, a narrow lane leads to Victoria Park (*P*20c), where Walk 20 ends. But for the moment keep ahead down to the sea, turning right past Crocodile Port and continuing through pines along the **Cap**

Spring fields near Alcúdia

d'es Pinar★ headland. The road soon starts to wind uphill and then turns up sharp right to climb the last few bends to the Ermita de la Victoria★ (172km ⚓🏠🅟🅿20a, 20b), where Walk 20 begins. Visit the old church and the viewpoint (walk down some steps to the left of the church and go straight along a narrow path). The restaurant here must have one of the most privileged positions on the island; its terrace overlooks the wide bay — a wonderful place to dine on a summer evening, when the lights of the port twinkle over the dark bay.

Back at the traffic lights, we now turn left down a straight road, soon coming into **Port d'Alcúdia** (180km ▲✕⊕), famous for the freshly-caught lobsters and other seafoods available in most of the beach-side restaurants. Straight ahead lies the commercial port, where ferries to Menorca and France dock in the deep harbour. Turn right to skirt the bay, where kilometres of white sandy beach stretch out in front of hotels, sun-clubs, and souvenir shops. Further along, keep left at the roundabout, to continue along the C712 between a string of hotels and holiday apartments, following the signposts to Ca'n Picafort. After a long straight stretch of road, at the second traffic light (185km) turn right where a sign indicates 'Sa Pobla'. This narrow road winds its way across the marshlands of S'Albufera (Car tour 4), passing by Alcúdia's electricity station and then through farmlands, to **Sa Pobla**, an agricultural town benefitting from extremely fertile soil. From here fruit and vegetables, especially potatoes, are exported all over Europe. Keep ahead through the town, and then turn right on the PM343, following signs to Palma.

Further on, go round to the right, and then take a left on the PM342, eventually coming to a roundabout. Go left here, on the C713 for Palma. One final visit is a 'must', however, before we return to the capital: at the next junction, turn right along a fairly rough road, following signs to the **Coves de Campanet★** (202km). These fabulous underground halls are resplendent with dramatically-lighted stalactites and stalagmites, and cannot be missed! Then maybe enjoy a drink on the terrace before returning to the C713. A straight run (ample 🚏) would take you back to Palma after 240km. But if you have time in hand, consider taking a detour from Inca, via Lloseta (where Walk 8 ends) to Alaró and the beautiful Orient valley (**P**7, 8; photographs pages 93, 96, 98), where Walks 7 and 8 begin. Alternatively, if you're running late, pick up the motorway at Inca.

4 VILLAGES OFF THE BEATEN TRACK, AND THE 'FAR EAST'

Palma • Sineu • Maria de la Salut • Santa Margalida • Ca'n Picafort • S'Albufera • Colònia de Sant Pere • Artà • Cala Rajada • Capdepera • Coves d'Artà • Sant Llorenç • Manacor • Petra • Sant Joan • Algaida • Palma

236km/146mi; 6h driving

On route: ⌂ at S'Albufera; Picnics (see pages 10-16): 4a, 4b, (21); Walks: 4a, 4b, (21)

Best to start out early if you want to complete this tour in one day, otherwise it is an ideal two-day programme, allowing more time for visits. Most of the roads are in good condition, although between Petra and Algaida we travel on little-used country lanes.

Opening hours/market days

The reception at the **S'Albufera** marshlands is open from 09.00-13.00 and 14.00-17.00 in winter and 14.00-19.00 in summer.

The **Museo Arqueológico** at Artà opens daily from 10.00-18.00.

The **Coves (Caves) d'Artà** are open daily from 10.00-17.00 in winter and 10.00-19.00 in summer.

Markets — Sineu: Wednesday mornings; **Maria de la Salut:** Friday mornings; **Santa Margalida:** Tuesday and Saturday mornings; **Ca'n Picafort:** Tuesday afternoons; **Artà:** Tuesday mornings; **Sant Llorenç:** Thursday mornings; **Manacor:** Monday mornings; **Petra:** Wednesday mornings; **Algaida:** Friday mornings

Leave Palma either from the 'Avenidas' or the ring road ('Via Cintura') by taking the Manacor exit off the roundabout. Just past the roundabout keep left on the PM301-1, signposted to Sineu. Almost immediately we are out in the countryside, among almond fields, farmsteads and low hills. At 17km we pass the turn-off left to Santa Eugénia (*P*4a, 4b; Walks 4a, 4b), after which the wide road (PMV310-1, later the PMV311-1) affords lovely views of the rolling countryside.

Come into the agricultural village of **Sineu** (33km ✦✗⊟), but do *not* follow signs to the right. Instead, when you come to the end of the road at the 'Stop' sign, turn down left; this will take you through the older part of the village (as well as passing the turn-off left to the petrol station, should you need it). Sineu, named Sixneu in Arabic

Palma at twilight

times and Sinium by the Romans, holds a lively agricultural market on Wednesday mornings, a tradition kept from as far back as the Middle Ages. Nowadays, not only will you find animals and stalls piled high with fresh vegetables and fruit, but almost anything that can be sold, from delicate porcelains to hand-embroidered shawls, copper pots, leatherware, shoes, etc. The ambience is one of rural charm, and people visit from all over the island. Keep on to the end of the village, and go right where you see a sign to 'Maria'. At the end, go right if you wish to visit the market square or turn left to continue the tour: you will cross a road and come to a roundabout, beyond which you keep straight ahead on the PM351 towards Maria.

This pleasant bucolic run over undulating countryside makes a change from the mountainous routes we have been following in previous tours. Soon we come to a small country village, **Maria de la Salut** (40km ♖⊕), completely hidden from the whirlwinds of tourism. These lands once belonged to the infamous Ramón Zaforteza, whose cruelty earned him the name 'Evil Count'. The local church has an interesting baroque bell tower. On entering the village, we turn left onto the PM352, following the signs to Santa Margalida (Margarita). Out in the country again, at the next junction (43km) we turn left on the PM334 to **Santa Margalida** (46km ♖), an ancient settlement inhabited both by Romans and Arabs, set on a low rise with excellent views of the distant sierra. At the roundabout, keep right, following signs to Ca'n Picafort along the PM341.

Coming over the top of the rise, we now have wonderful views of the wide bay of Alcúdia, with the Cap d'es Pinar (Car tour 3) on the left horizon and the Artà mountains off to the right. Come to **Ca'n Picafort** (56km ⛰△✕⛱⊕), where a long wide beach stretches out, bordered by miles of sand dunes, and a tiled esplanade shaded by many multi-coloured sun umbrellas offers the choice of count-less sea-front cafés. To visit the **Albufera** marshlands (a 'must' for nature-lovers, turn left at the main road (C712) and drive as far as the little bridge (Es Pont dels Inglesos), where you will find the entrance on the left. It's about 1km along the lane to the reception area — either drive or walk to it; entrance is free. Many footpaths cross the reeded marshes, with several 'hides' at strategic points — a bird-watchers' paradise! Some of the resident marsh-dwellers you might see are crakes, terns, warblers or hoopoes, and sandpipers, as well as egrets or wagtails in winter, together with migrating herons or cranes. Kestrels, ospreys and marsh harriers also abound, as do many others. There are orchids here, too, and a multitude of colourful wild flowers in spring. Near the reception, a museum with audiovisual effects is extremely interesting.

Back in Ca'n Picafort, turn down towards the sea at the far end of the resort and follow the sign to Son Baulo, going right at the end of the road. Just past a large hotel, you can park and walk down onto the beach by the side of a lagoon. Continuing to the right, along sandy trails over the dunes, you will come to a well-preserved prehistoric settlement on a small headland — a fascinating place.

We leave Ca'n Picafort now, coming back onto the C712 and turning left towards Artà along a wide road across open countryside. We pass by a road off left to Son Serra de la Marina (a characterless waterfront mass of chalets) and a road off right to Petra (🚻 at 71km). At 73km turn left on the PM333-1, soon coming to the **Colònia de Sant Pere** (78km 🏨🛉△🍴), the last little enclave on the eastern side of Alcúdia bay. There's a small beach, but not much else, so keep ahead on the road, past orchards and bright smallholdings, towards **The Creek**, a waterfront village, and **Betlem**, a residential area set on the rocks, with the stark backdrop of the Artà range reflecting in the deep blue waters. Here the tarmac ends, but a sandy trail goes on for a couple of kilometres — a beautiful coastal walk through pine woods, ending at a rocky cove; there is also a rocky trail down to two hidden beaches near the start of the track.

Returning to the C712, we turn left to continue over a mountainous landscape to **Artà** (96km 🛉🅿🍴🚻⊕M). There is quite a lot to see here, so you will need to spend some time. On entering the town, keep straight ahead, following signs to the 'Ermita', then turning left in the square. You soon come out of the town, climbing a tarmac country lane up into the desolate hills for some 9km (the last 4km are narrow and winding). We come to S'Ermita de Betlem (106km 🛉📷), a sanctuary set on a mountaintop in the middle of nowhere. Here a silent cypress-lined avenue leads up to the hermitage, instilling peace into the soul. To find the best viewpoint, go to the left of the building and through the small gate at the back, to follow a stony trail over the brow of the mountain for stunning views down over the wide bay of Alcúdia and the distant rocky Formentor Peninsula, with the Colònia de Sant Pere and Betlem below on the coast. These mountains were once the private shooting grounds of the ancient kings of Mallorca.

Back in Artà, keep left up to the top of the hill to visit the Almudaina, the site of a Moorish fortress, where the Santuari de Sant Salvador still stands. You can walk round the parapets to admire the town from above. The archeological museum is also worth a visit; it contains many important pieces, including five bronze statuettes dating from the 2nd century BC. Finally, you won't want to miss a nearby prehistoric village: to get there, descend from the Almudaina and the church and turn left, following the narrow street to come out onto the C715 on the far side of town (115km), then turn left again: some 100m along, on a bend, lies the entrance to **Ses Paisses**★ (116km ⋔), where you can see the *talaiots* (stone structures) of an ancient civilisation.

Return to the C715 and turn right towards Cala Rajada, passing the turn off left to Cala Estreta (*P*21 and Walk 21) about 1km out of town. On approaching Capdepera, where a medieval fortress with parapets crowns the top of the hill, go left, skirting the village, to continue to **Cala Rajada** (133km ⛰✕⬛⊕), a picturesque fishing port on the easternmost tip of the island. To get to the beach (Cala Guya) keep left; for the port go right. It's definitely worth driving up the twisting road from the port to the lighthouse (134km 📷) for the views. Then take the road straight out and back to **Capdepera** (142km ⛺⬛✕⊕); here you can

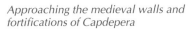

Approaching the medieval walls and fortifications of Capdepera

walk around the parapets for panoramic views over Cala Rajada and the pine-wooded coast, or visit the small oratory inside the wall built by King Sancho during the 14th century.

From Capdepera, we now follow signs to Canyamel along the PM404. At 145km take the turn-off left to the 'Coves d Artà' *(not easily seen until you are on top of it).* After a short way along a straight stretch of road, we turn left again, on the PMV4042; this winds up to the **Coves d'Artà★** (152km 📷). An impressive stone stairway leads us into a huge black hole under the cliff — our journey into these fantastic underground halls, once the hideout of pirates, has begun. It will take us through an unreal landscape of thousands of cleverly-lit stalactites and stalagmites, and eerie caverns of imposing grandeur.

After this impressive visit, our eyes readjusting once more to the daylight, we go back down the road, keeping straight ahead to the turn-off left (157km) signposted to Canyamel. Soon we pass the **Torre de Canyamel** (158km ✕; photograph and notes page 62). Further along, go left at the roundabout, to come to the **Platja de Canyamel** (162km ▲✕), a beautiful wide sandy bay, bordered on either side by high pine-covered cliffs.

Doubling back on our tracks, we return to the junction and keep straight ahead towards Artà, then go left at the roundabout back onto the PM404. After the tunnel, a straight run brings us to **Son Servera** (165km ✝🛒⊕), where we keep straight up the hill and then turn right on the PM403. Another straight road takes us into **Sant Llorenç d'es Cardassar** (172km ✝✕⊕), an agricultural village. Once through the centre we meet the C715, where we turn left.

From here it's another 6km (🛒 at 174km) to **Manacor** (180km ✝▲✕🛒⊕M), the second largest town on Mallorca, mostly industrial. It is the centre for hand-carved furniture, and there are good ceramic shops — as well as

Fishing nets drying near the cathedral in Palma make a colourful display.

the world-famous 'Majorica' pearl factory, visited daily by coachloads of tourists. In 1229, when Jaime I took Manacor back from the Moors, there was even a mosque and several noble Arab dwellings in this town.

Continuing along the C715, we soon turn off right (184km) onto the PM332, signposted to Petra; this is a quieter country road. At 191km, on coming to a round-about, go left into **Petra** (192km ♣☎⊕M), birthplace of Fray Juniper Serra, the Franciscan monk who founded many missions in North America — missions which later became great cities such as San Diego and San Francisco (there is a bust comemmorating this in Washington DC). It is a little difficult to find his house of birth (with museum) in the labyrinth of narrow streets: to get there, follow the signs to Sant Joan, pass a church, and then turn left; you will come to a narrow street on the left with a 'No Entry' sign. The house is just along this street, but the key is at No 2 Calle Miguel de Petra (the road you are on). Un-fortunately there is not much room to leave your car, but you should be able to park beyond house No 2, just after the road turns left.

Our homeward route now leaves Petra along an old country lane (PM322), crossing a lonely landscape of agricultural fields and low hills, eventually coming to **Sant Joan** (201km ⊕), where a popular *romería* is celebrated just before Easter, the 'Festival of Bread and Fishes', and the local housewives bake home-made fish pasties. Do *not* follow the signs to Palma, but turn up right, and then go left, following the signs to Pina. At the junction outside Sant Joan keep straight ahead along the PM323. Driving into the sunset, we now follow this winding country lane over an undulating and peaceful landscape, thus avoiding the busy C715 for a little longer. At the next junction, keep left towards Algaida (signposted).

At 215km, on the outskirts of **Algaida** (♣✕☎⊕), you pick up the C715, for a straight run (ample ✕☎) back to Palma's ring road (236km).

5 THE ROUTE OF CAVES AND MONASTERIES

Palma • Manacor • Coves dels Hams • Reserva Africana • Porto Cristo • Coves del Drac • Calas de Mallorca • Porto Colom • Santuari de Sant Salvador • Felanitx • Castell de Santueri • Cala d'Or • Porto Petro • Santanyí • Cala Figuera • Ses Salines • Colònia de Sant Jordi • Campos • Santuari de Monti-Sion • Porreres • Palma

255km/158mi; 6h driving (a two-day tour)

On route: ♨ at the Coves dels Hams, Coves del Drac and Santuari de Sant Salvador

You could do this tour in one day, but there would not be sufficient time to visit all the interesting places on route; the caves are considered one of the natural wonders of the world, and to appreciate the African Reserve you'll want to take your time. I suggest you spend the night at a mountain-top monastery high above these landscapes, where monks straight out of the Middle Ages — with long white beards and wearing brown hooded robes — glide silently between the sanctuary walls; it is quite an experience. Hence, we'll make this a two-day programme — have fun!

Opening hours/market days
The **Santuari de Sant Salvador** (for overnight stay tel: 827282) is best booked in advance in summer, otherwise just book in at the souvenir shop on arrival. The monastery is open daily, but doors close at 23.00.
The **Coves dels Hams** are open daily from 10.30-13.15 and 14.15-17.30; there is a tour (with concert) every 20 minutes.
The **Reserva Africana** (safari park) is open daily from 09.00-17.00 in winter and from 09.00-19.00 in summer.
The **Coves del Drac** are open daily. There is a tour with concert at 12.00, 14.00, 15.30 and 16.30 (no concert) in winter; in summer there is a tour with concert every hour from 10.00-17.00.
The **Acuario de Mallorca** opens daily from 11.00-15.00 in winter and from 10.00-18.30 in summer.
The **'Exotic Parque' Los Pájaros** opens daily from 10.00-19.00.
Markets — Manacor: Monday mornings; **Felanitx:** Sunday mornings; **Santanyí:** Saturday mornings; **Colònia Sant Jordi:** Wednesday mornings; **Campos:** Thursday mornings; **Porreres:** Tuesday mornings; **Montuïri:** Monday mornings

Leave Palma either from the 'Avenidas' or the ring road ('Via Cintura') by taking the Manacor exit off the roundabout. Following the C715 through beautiful open countryside, you pass Algaida (21km ♦✖♣⊕) and Montuïri (28km ✖⊕) and then drive through **Vilafranca de Bonany** (38km ✖♣⊕). More rolling green hills accompany you to the island's second largest town, **Manacor** (46km ♦▲✖ ♣⊕M; see Car tour 4). Keep straight ahead, and then turn right at the sign to Porto Cristo, following more 'Porto Cristo' signs through the town's wide palm-lined avenues.

   Out in the country again, follow the PM402 (✖ at 53km, ♣ at 56km). At 58km (✖) turn in right along a tree-lined entrance to the **Coves dels Hams★**. Time to stretch our legs here, on a visit to these magnificent subterranean hallways and underground lakes, discovered only in the early 1900s by a Mallorcan speleologist. Afterwards have morning coffee at the open-air café.

Back on the road, turn right now for Porto Cristo, and on entering the town (visited later in the tour) go left at the roundabout, following signs to Son Servera. You come onto the PMV402-3 — the road to the safari park (several ✕). Pass by the turn-offs to Cala Moreia and S'Illot, and turn left at the signpost 'Safari', coming to the **Reserva Africana★** (65km). This is an auto-safari, and you can either drive your own car or take the little train; it's a real thrill to see so many animals — rhinos, elephants, ostriches, giraffes, hippos, monkeys, crocodiles and many, many more. The children will love it. There are also elephant shows twice a day.

We return after this exciting 'memory of Africa' to **Porto Cristo** (70km ▲▲✕), thought to be an important sea port in Roman times. Keep straight on at the roundabout for 'Playa' and 'Port', and then go right down a steep hill, coming to the picturesque fishing port and beach. There is quite a good parking area here (just down left below the small esplanade), if you wish to explore. There are also boat trips from the jetty, though I doubt you will have time to fit this in too.

Continuing, follow the 'Cuevas del Drach' signposting, coming to the **Coves del Drac★** (72km) just outside Porto Cristo. The Archduke Luis Salvador of Austria (see pages 24 and 87) discovered these caves on his extensive travels on Mallorca and commissioned the French geologist, Martel, to explore them and and map them out. The hour-long guided tour takes us through a labyrinth of stone corridors, steps, and brilliantly-illuminated caverns, and ends with the mystical strains of violins drifting across the still waters of an underground lake reflecting a thousand stalactites... a floating concert. Nearby, the **Acuario de Mallorca** makes another colourful and fascinating visit, where you'll see exotic fish from the Australian coral reef, dreaded piranhas from Brazil, and Mediterranean sharks.

Return to the main road and turn left towards the 'Calas de Mallorca' along the PMV401-4, a country lane that runs parallel with the coast through almond orchards and open fields. At 79km, pass by the turn-off to Cala Romántica (✕) — another pretty cove. Soon we turn left again on a rough road signposted 'Calas de Mallorca' and, just here on the left, is the **'Exotic Parque' Los Pájaros**★ (84km). Here you can see all kinds of beautiful cactii, tropical plants and a multitude of exotic birds of many colours.

Keeping along the road bordered by rough low scrub, we soon arrive at the unpreposessing **Calas de Mallorca** (88km ▲▲ ✖) — just a clump of ugly hotels sitting ostentatiously on the rocks and looking terribly out of place. One wonders why it was ever allowed to be built. However, the best 'view' can be had by turning left at the sign to the Hotel Sol Canarios and driving down the dirt track to the point where it bends down right towards the cove. Here you can walk over the rocky headland to the left, to find an untouched part of the coastline, even though the opposite side of the main *cala* is heavily burdened with holiday chalets and high-rise hotel blocks.

Back on the road, go left just by the Hotel Sol Canarios and, after the bend, you will see a road off right, signposted to Cala Murada. Follow this road out of the Calas, rising and dropping sharply over the hills; it's just like being on the big dipper! When you come to a 'Stop' sign at the end, go left and follow what seems like an endless (and signpostless) run. Eventually you will come to **Cala Murada** (97km ▲▲ ✖), a small bay with a sandy cove, also blighted with characterless building developments, although the beach is quite pleasant.

Return along the same road, continuing straight ahead at the junction. When you rejoin the PMV401-4, turn left. At the end, go left again on the PM401 (✖), to come to **Porto Colom** (106km ▲▲ ✖), a centuries-old commercial and fishing port, now also a residential area and summer resort popular among the Mallorcans. You can drive round the bay, over to Cala Marçal (where there is a good beach). Or head back along the quayside, and then turn right on the PM406, signposted 'Far' (lighthouse); this narrow tarmac lane rounds the port, with picturesque views of fishing schooners and boat-houses, and climbs to the lighthouse on the headland, with panoramic views over the port (📷).

Return to the PM401 and head towards Felanitx, but turn off left just before the town (123km, signposted 'Sant Salvador'). This winding road climbs the steep slopes to the **Santuari de Sant Salvador**★ (128km ▮▲✖⊞📷) at a height of 510m/1675ft, with its impressive 360° panoramas. An enormous monument (37m/120ft high) dominates the car park. A short walk takes us up to the monastery buildings, where a valuable Gothic altarpiece can be seen encased in glass. Enquiries for your overnight stay can be

Near Alquería Blanca the soil supports a double crop: barley is planted in the orchards, below the fig trees.

made at the souvenir shop — imagine waking up to these panoramic views with tomorrow's rising sun!

Day two: After breakfast, leave the monastery to wind back down to the PM401 and turn left to come into **Felanitx** (134km), a wine-making town, also famous for its ceramics. Its church is built of the same honey-coloured stone as Palma's cathedral. Follow signs to Palma, going right at the first roundabout and left at the second, along palm-lined avenues. Drive through the town guided by the 'Santanyí' signs, to come out of Felanitx on the Carrer de Santueri (C714). On a bend (137km), turn left on a narrow country lane winding through fruit orchards, orange groves and vineyards, up to the **Castell de Santueri★** (142km ∎▣). This castle was reconstructed over the remains of a Moorish stronghold during the 13th century — certainly a very strategic position. In summer, the door is open and on payment of a small fee, you can walk around the remaining fortress walls, with stunning views on all sides.

Back down the lane, we rejoin the C714, going left for 'Cala d'Or', then left again along the PMV401-6. After passing through the hamlet of **Es Carritxó**, we climb over the hills to **Calonge** (♦✕), beyond which we turn left again to **Cala d'Or** (152km ▲✕▭⊕). This dazzling-white summer resort straddles aquamarine and turquoise-hued coves, where sandy beaches hide. Visit the marina, where expensive yachts and fishing boats bob up and down on the deep blue sea, or take refreshments at one of the waterside cafés . From Cala d'Or follow the signs to nearby **Porto Petro** (157km ♦▲✕), another attractive little harbour, quieter than Cala d'Or.

From Porto Petro, take the road signposted to Santanyí (✕ at 161km), coming to **Alquería Blanca** (163km ♦). Here keep straight up the main road, to join the C717, and turn left. At 165km we pass a lane up right to the Ermita de la Consolación, a small 17th-century oratory, and soon after we arrive at **Santanyí** (168 km ♦✕▭⊕). Follow the signs to Cala Figuera through the town, eventually coming out onto the PMV610-2, which will take us to **Cala Figuera**

42

Winter's changeable weather paints a dramatic canvas — especially when watchtowers or windmills are seen in silhouette.

(173km 🏔️ ✕). Scene of many an onslought by pirates and Saracens in the past, it must surely be one of the prettiest *calas* in Mallorca. Drive down to the 'Port', and park on the slope; the rest of the way is pedestrianised. Picturesque views over fishing boats moored in the cove can be enjoyed by continuing uphill on foot, or stretch your legs along the rocky headland.

Back along the PMV610-2, we can discover the pretty palm-shaded beach of Cala Santanyí by turning left (signposted); it lies a couple of kilometres down a rough lane. From this small cove follow the sign for Palma, coming back onto the PMV610-2, and heading left back into Santanyí. Drive straight through the town, now following the signs to Ses Salines. Coming out onto the PM610, we pass the turn-off to Cala S'Almonia and Cala Llombarts at 183km (the blowhole at Cala S'Almonia is fascinating to watch on a rough day). Just past this turn-off, we pass through **Es Llombarts** (184km ✕). Straight on out of the village, keep your eye on the Ses Salines signs, passing the turn-off left (186km) to 'Cap Salines' and its lighthouse, on the southernmost tip of the island. Come to **Ses Salines** (187km ✕🍽️⊕), an agricultural village. There are remains of several prehistoric talayotic settlements here, as well as Roman tombs scattered about from here as far as the coast. Go through the village and head left at the roundabout, to continue along the PM610 to the **Colònia de Sant Jordi** (194km 🏔️✕🍽️⊕). Go straight ahead at the roundabout, pass the petrol station, then turn left to find a parking area by the beach. Boats leave here for the isle of Cabrera in summer (a sometimes choppy crossing across the deep channel). Apart from the seafront restaurants, the real attractions here are the long white sandy beaches reached on foot, further round the bay.

Leaving the colony behind, we return to the roundabout and go left on the PM604 for a straight run (✕ at 199km) to **Campos** (207km ⚓✕🍽️⊕), a town dating from the 1300s. No less than five watchtowers were built in Campos during the 14th century! The church boasts an original

43

Farm near Ses Salines

painting by the Spanish artist, Murillo, which originally hung in the Sant Blai hermitage nearby. Apart from this, Campos is basically an agricultural centre and does not have a great deal to offer the tourist.

Keep left, straight through the town, and then veer right at the second petrol station, following signposting to Porreres. Cross over the road at the 'Stop' sign, to follow a pleasant country run along the PM504. At the next junction go left and follow the pink signpost to 'Monti-Sion' along the PM503. After about 1km, turn left again, to climb the low hill (turning left twice) up to the **Santuari de Monti-Sion** (218 km ✝▲✕☺). Admire the far-reaching views down over the fertile plain, before climbing the steps to enter the peaceful courtyard with its Gothic-style stone archways and central well.

Back on the PM503, turn left, then right, into **Porreres** (221km ✝➟⊕), a wine-producing centre and agricultural village, not terribly on the tourist wavelength. Keep ahead into the centre and then go left on the PM503 for Montuïri. You pick up the C715, turning left for a straight run (ample ✕➟) back to Palma's ring road (255km).

6 SOUTHERN RESORTS AND THE PUIG DE RANDA

**Palma • Es Molinar • Coll d'en Rabassa • Ca'n Pastilla •
S'Arenal • Cap Blanc • Cala Pí • Capocorp Vell •
S'Estanyol • Ses Covetes and Es Trenc • Campos •
Llucmajor • Puig de Randa and Santuari de Cura • Palma**

132km/82mi; 4h driving

On route: ⊞ at the Santuari de Cura; Picnic 22 (page16); Walk 22

*Although there is less of touristic interest on this car tour, it is ideal
for the summer, as it leads to several beautiful beaches. We end up
at the Puig de Randa, from where the whole of our itinerary is
captured in a magnificent view over the coast.*

Opening hours/market days
Capocorp Vell (megalithic village) is open daily from 10.00-18.00;
it closes a little earlier in winter and is also closed on Thursdays
during the winter.

Markets — Campos: Thursday mornings; **Llucmajor:** Wednesday
and Sunday mornings

Leave Palma from the eastern end of the 'Avenidas', going
left towards 'Platja de Palma', and turn off right to **Es
Molinar** at the traffic light. The road rounds a charming
little fishing port, and at the end you can turn right for the
sea-front. Here, overlooking Palma Bay, we have the
famous Portixol restaurant, popular for its wonderful fresh
seafood dishes. We can only drive a little way along the
front, past 'olde world'-style terraced houses, then must
head back onto the main road. There are also some very
good seafood restaurants at **Coll d'en Rabassa** (5km ✕) —
and the lovely wide sandy beach of Ciutat Jardí ('City
Garden'), mostly visited by Palma city-dwellers. Back on
the main road, we continue up through the shopping area
and, at the last set of traffic lights, turn right (signposted to
Ca'n Pastilla). Soon after passing the electricity plant, we
come into **Ca'n Pastilla** (7km ▲✕➾⊕). Here the tourist
resort begins and, edged by miles of wide sandy beach,
stretches out all the way to S'Arenal, with plenty of shops
to browse through and a myriad of sea-front cafés.

At the end of Ca'n Pastilla, turn left, then right, to
continue on the long road that runs behind a string of
hotels, restaurants, barbecue stalls and holiday blocks (as
the main part of the sea-front has been pedestrianised).
However, towards the end of **S'Arenal** (13km ▲✕➾⊕),
we can turn right down any of the side streets, to come to
the beach, then continue along the front all the way to the
end. Here go up the steepish slope of the Carrer Sant
Bartolomé (signposted 'Cala Blava'). At the top, keep right,
along the middle of the three roads, past more hotels. At
the roundabout, go right again along the PM601-4 towards

45

Cala Blava. This road escapes into the countryside between low pines and scrub. Soon we'll come to a sign to
Cala Blava off right but, to avoid a boring drive around the
residential area with no apparent access to the little cove,
keep left along the PM601-4, across a rather desolate
landscape of low scrub, where not even agriculture has
disturbed the land (▲▲✗ at 17km). At 19km, just past the
Maori Hotel, a rough road goes off right to the cliff-edge
— a popular area for *parapenta* enthusiasts. We pass
various residential areas — Sa Torre, Bahía Azul, Bahía
Grande and El Dorado and, after a long stretch of cliff-top
road, we come to the lighthouse at **Cap Blanc** (31km 📷),
the 'White Cape'. There is also a 16th-century watchtower
to the left of the lighthouse, unfortunately inside the military zone. But it's lovely to walk along the cliff-tops and,
if the weather is clear, you can see the isle of Cabrera on
the distant blue horizon.

From Cap Blanc the road swings inland and heads once
more into open country. At 37km we turn off right towards
Cala Pí. A rough narrow road takes us across miles of dry
scrubland to the beautiful creek of **Cala Pí** (41km ▲▲✗;
photograph page 136), where a lovely beach hides
between the cliffs. Drive to the end of the road, and park
by the watchtower or just before it. Then find the steps
down to the creek. Fishing boats share the narrow inlet
with expensive white yachts, and fishermen's cottages
reflect in the turquoise waters. You'll also spot some caves
in the cliff-side opposite. Even if you don't have time for
all of Walk 22 today, do at least visit Cala Beltrán (*P*22).

Back at the junction (46km) we turn right, after 500m
coming to the megalithic village of **Capocorp Vell★** (🏛;
see notes and photograph opposite). From here continue
towards S'Estanyol (✗ at 47km and 51km). At the next
junction, turn right on the PMV601-5, after another straight
run entering the uninspiring resort of **S'Estanyol** (58km ✗).
Keep straight on down to the seafront. Turn left, past a
string of characterless houses facing the rocky sea-front,
and eventually come to **Sa Rápita** (61km ✗) , where the
Marina Yacht Club seems to be the only sign of life.

We meet the PM603 and leave the coast, out in the
country once more. At 63km turn right for Ses Covetes; this
narrow country lane meanders between old stone farmhouses where prickly pear cacti ramble at random. About
1km along, go right again, following a wider road back to
the coast and **Ses Covetes** (65km ✗). At the end of the road
go right; you can park further along, by the chained-off

Pristine Es Trenc beach (top), colourful fields at Ses Covetes (middle), and Capocorp Vell (bottom). Important excavations at Capocorp Vell uncovered many valuable pieces, remains of a settlement of some 3000 years ago. Althoughthe 'finds' are now in Barcelona's Archeological Museum and the site has unfortunately been 'tarted up' for tourists (completely destroying its natural charm), a scramble among these talayotic ruins and stone chambers affords an imaginative insight into Bronze Age communities of the past.

gateway to the beach — a lovely long and white sandy stretch not often crowded, even in summer. If it's hot, you'll want to swim, or have a meal at the Ran de Mar restaurant (very good *paella*). Alternatively, go back to the road, and head off right onto the other side of the headland, past half-finished beach chalets, to find the virgin beach of **Es Trenc**. This Carribean-like beach stretches out for miles below the sand dunes, and as yet is relatively unspoilt, apart from the ugly kiosk near the beginning. Further round the bay, naturists bathe in paradisial surroundings.

Back on asphalt and heading away from the coast once more, keep straight on along country lanes, following the signs to Palma and Campos, going left at 70km. At 72km turn right on the PM603. In **Campos** (77km ✚✕🚌⊕; Car tour 5) turn left, then head straight through the town for 'Palma'. At the main road (C717; 🚌), turn left for Llucmajor. This good, wide road through open countryside brings us to **Llucmajor** (89km ✝✗🍽⊕M), where the 17th-century convent of Bonaventura and the 18th-century church are the main architectural highlights. By the C717, on the outskirts of the village, a stone cross indicates the site of a confrontation between the troops of Jaime III and the army of Pedro IV of Aragón. Leave Llucmajor from the first roundabout, turning right up the street where the Tiá Taleca restaurant is on the corner, and follow the signs 'Travesía' through the town (towards Algaida).

You come out on the Algaida road, the PM501, once more in the countryside. At 95km turn off right up a narrow lane into **Randa** (96km ✝✗), a small hillside village. Driving slowly up the narrow street, turn left just past the restaurant and then go right almost immediately, following signs 'Santuari de Cura' past the elegant Es Racó restaurant and hotel. The road winds up the **Puig de Randa** in a series of tight bends, passing the entrance to the Santuari de Gràcia (✝🏠), founded in the Middle Ages and once a travellers' hostel. Set under the brow of an enormous escarpment, it makes a beautiful setting for the open-air concerts held on some summer evenings. But it is best to visit on your way down, if it's late in the day and you want to get to the top to see the view before dusk. We pass another small oratory on the ascent — Sant Honorat, on the right.

Finally, at a height of 548m/1800ft, we arrive at the **Santuari de Cura★** (101km ✝▲✗🎍🏠M). Visits to the library and small chapel are a must. The ancient library contains many manuscripts, prayer books and other relics from the days of the 13th-century scholar, Ramon Llull, who was born shortly after the Reconquest of Mallorca. But apart from the historical value of the visit, there are captivating views on all sides — the southern coast with the beautiful beaches we have just visited, Cap Blanc, the mountains of Llevant and the monastery at Felanitx, the wide central plain, dotted with countless towns and villages, and the long chain of the Serra de Tramuntana closing off the northern horizon — all the various settings of our earlier car tours around the island. Alcúdia's bay is also visible on a clear day, as is the mystical isle of Cabrera to the south. Let's treat ourselves to a sundowner on the terrace, surrounded by these magnificent panoramas!

Once back in Randa, turn right on the PM501, to drive through more low hills to **Algaida** (111km ✝✗🍽⊕). Follow the signs to Palma through the village, turning left on the C715 for a straight run (ample ✗🍽) to the city (132km).

❀ Walking

This new edition of *Landscapes of Mallorca* covers about 350km (over 200 miles) of some of the best walking on Mallorca. I have included several new and exciting walks in a variety of landscapes, while omitting walks which became 'spoiled' over the years for one reason or another. Several good new short walks have been introduced as well, to encourage beginners to take up this wonderful pastime.

I hope you'll also use this book, together with the bus, train and boat timetables on pages 137-139, to make up your own walk combinations. I've indicated where routes link up on the walking maps, and the pull-out touring map shows the general location of all the walks. One word of caution. *Never try to get from one walk to another on uncharted terrain!* Only combine walks by following paths described in these notes or by using roads or tracks: don't try to cross rough country (which might prove dangerous) or private land (where you may not have right of way).

There are walks in the book for everyone.

Beginners: Start on the walks graded 'easy' — and be sure to check all the short and alternative versions of the main walks; these are often suggestions for easier rambles. The picnic suggestions all describe superb easy walks.

Experienced walkers: If you are used to rough terrain and have a head for heights, you should be able to tackle almost all the walks in the book (a few are recommended for experts only). Naturally, you will take into account the weather conditions and their consequences. For example, if it has been raining recently, some of the mountain walks will be unsuitable. Also, ***storm damage can make the way unsafe at any time.*** Remember, too, always to follow the route as described in this book. If you have not reached one of the landmarks after a reasonable time, you *must* go back to the last 'sure' point and start again.

Experts: All the walks described are suitable for you — provided you always use extreme caution.

Guides, waymarking, maps

A couple of walks are graded as suitable for experts only, and I recommend that anyone other than an expert walker hire a **guide** for these routes. Not because they are particularly difficult, but because you could be suddenly overtaken by thick mists and get lost or, due to poor way-marking, you could miss the path and find yourselves in a potentially hazardous position. Guides are not easily found on the island, but you could contact: Mauricio Espinar, Carrer Almirall Cervera 23, Port de Pollença; tel: 531030. He speaks fluent English and French and understands some German. Otherwise you can reach me at: Carrer de Ses Monges 9, 1°, Santa Eugènia 07142; tel: 144055.

Waymarking of walks is minimal. There is very little signposting. Many mountain routes were marked with red paint in years past (often hard to follow today); a few routes have been waymarked with paint more recently. Another form of waymarking is the cairn — a small pile of rocks. These are placed at intervals at various points along the way; after a while you'll become accustomed to keeping a lookout for these unusual mountain 'signs'.

The **maps** in this book have been adapted from the most recent 1:25,000 IGN and 1:50,000 military maps of the Balearics. You can buy them in advance from your usual map stockist or in Palma — either from the military head-quarters on the 'Rambla', or from the 'Armería', 7b Carrer Arquebisbe Asparreg.

R ight of way

Much of Mallorca is private land, and in recent years many landowners are attempting to close off routes, or parts of routes, previously open to walkers. While one can understand and sympathise with the problem of carelessly-dropped litter, open gates or uprooted crops, there does seem to be a feeling of the sierra being gradually 'closed off' — only to be enjoyed by a privileged few. Many of the routes involved are ancient pilgrims' trails, herding routes or wayfarers' roads connecting mountain villages — routes that have been freely accessible for hundreds of years.

In 1996 the ADIM (Association for the Defense of Itin-eraries in Mallorca) was formed to protect walkers' rights of way; see page 144, if you would like to join. In the mean-time, you should not have any problems with the routes described in this book, and I ask you to walk so respectfully that landowners will not even notice your passing.

W hat to take

If you're already on Mallorca when you find this book, and you haven't any special equipment such as a rucksack, boots or a torch, you can still do some of the walks — or buy yourself some equipment at one of the sports shops on the island. Don't attempt the more difficult walks without the proper equipment! For each walk in the book, the *minimum* equipment is listed. Where walking boots are required, there is, unfortunately, no substitute: you will need to rely on the grip and ankle support they provide (many island trails are stony), as well as their waterproof qualities (in winter and spring some normally-dry streams are in flow). All other walks should be made with stout shoes, preferably with thick rubber soles, to grip on wet or slippery surfaces.

You may find the following checklist useful:

comfortable walking boots	up-to-date transport timetables
waterproof rain gear	plastic bottle, purifying tablets
long-sleeved shirt (sun protection)	long trousers, tight at the ankles
bandages, plasters, etc	suncream, sunglasses
plastic plates, cups, etc	knives, openers, string
anorak, two light cardigans	insect repellant
extra pair of socks and shoelaces	sunhat, plastic rainhat
small rucksack	torch, whistle, compass
plastic groundsheet	first-aid kit, safety pins, etc

Please bear in mind that I've not done *every* walk in this book under *all* weather conditions, and I may not realise just how hot — or wet — some walks might be. Your good judgement will help you to modify the equipment list according to the season.

Weather

The weather on Mallorca can be quite variable. It can be very cold in winter — but not necessarily so. In fact, some winters are pleasantly mild. It is swelteringly hot and humid from July to September. The most unreliable months are March/April and September/October, when the capricious spring and autumn rains arrive.

Most people will find it far too hot in summer for any of the strenuous walks in this book. But two of the walks, both strenuous, generally *must* be done in summer: Walk 10 (from the Mirador de Ses Barques to Sa Calobra) and Walk 11 (the Torrent de Pareis — only negotiable after a long period without rain) both rely on the Sa Calobra boat connection.*

Generally the **best walking months** are January and February, perhaps March and April — if it's not too wet, May and early June, September and October — likewise,

*This boat also operates all through the winter *if the weather is good*. Telephone 'Tramuntana Boats' (633109) to see if the boat is running during your visit to the island.

if it's not too wet!, November and December. These are rough guidelines, and it sometimes seems that every year proves to be an exception! Freak weather, with heavy snow on the sierra, is not unknown in May...

A weather report with meteorological maps is given in the daily newspapers and on television every evening following the main news. You can also telephone for 'Información Meteorológica' 24 hours a day (tel: 094). But be warned: the recorded message is in Spanish, and you may have to ask someone to interpret for you.

Dogs and other nuisances

You'll encounter **dogs** at all the farms, almost always chained up. It is a good idea for each walker always to carry a stout stick, but *never* wave the stick about to menace the dogs. Moreover, always go *quietly* through all private land, leaving gates *exactly* as you find them. Only resort to your stick when confronted by an unchained and obviously unfriendly dog. (If you wish to invest in an ultra-sonic dog deterrent, the Dog Dazer, contact Sunflower Books.) There are four types of **snakes** on the island, some of them growing to about 1-1.5 metres/yards long — but none is dangerous to man. We also have **scorpions**, but these are tiny (4 centimetres/1.5 inches). They might sting you, but you won't come to any harm. More troublesome are **mosquitos** and **ticks**. Always carry insect repellant and, when walking in dense undergrowth, it's always wise to wear long trousers, with your socks pulled up round the trouser legs, and a long-sleeved shirt.

Walkers' checklist

The following points cannot be stressed too often:
- **At any time a walk may become unsafe** due to heavy storms. If the route is not as described in this book, and your way ahead is not secure, do not attempt to go on.
- **Walks recommended for experts only** may be unsuitable in winter or after storms, or may be very wet after heavy rain. (In mild winters, all the walks are possible.)
- **Never walk alone**; four is the best walking group.
- **Do not overestimate your energies**; your speed will be determined by the slowest walker in your group.
- **Transport** connections at the end of a walk are vital.
- **Proper shoes** or boots are a necessity.
- **Mists** can suddenly appear on the higher mountains.
- **Warm clothing** is needed on the mountains; even in summer take some along, just in case you are delayed.

- **Compass, whistle, torch** weigh little, but might save your life.
- **Extra rations** must be taken on long walks.
- **Always take a sunhat** with you, and in summer a cover-up for your arms and legs as well.
- **A stout stick** is a help on rough terrain and for discouraging the rare unchained, menacing dog.
- **Do not panic** in an emergency.
- Read and re-read the *'Important note'* on page 2 and the country code on page 54, as well as guidelines on grade and equipment for each walk you plan to take.

Where to stay

Many people will be staying in or around Palma during their holiday on the island. From the capital a good public transport system permits daily travel to most parts of Mallorca. For this reason, all the walks are written up to include transport to and from Palma (however, timetables for buses from other holiday bases are also included).

Whereas the capital is your best choice if you're relying on public transport, if you plan to rent a car you have a far greater choice of locations — especially if you plan to take only short or easy walks.

If you intend to do a lot of hiking, remember that most of the island's best walks lie along the mountain chain stretching from Valldemossa to Pollença. Good centres for walks are therefore Sóller and its port and Pollença and its port. This is especially so in summer, when the bus is running at good intervals along the C710 mountain road between Sóller and Pollença (see Timetable 9, page 139); many of the walks then lie within easy reach.

Briefly, if you're planning to do a lot of walking, are *pre-booking a package holiday,* and will rely on public transport, **Palma** is your best centre. **Pollença** and **Sóller** (and their ports) are also good choices.

For those *not* booking 'all-in' holidays, there is the interesting alternative of staying at one of Mallorca's sanctuaries, many of which still run a hostelry.

Lluc, a large monastery steeped in history and set in romantic surroundings high in the mountains, is placed just at the centre of some of the best island walks. Visitors may stay overnight — or for as long as they wish — in the hostelry run by the friars. Buses connect Lluc with Palma direct and with Inca (from where there are hourly trains to Palma). There are also buses to Sóller and Pollença — so there's no need to feel 'cut off from civilisation'.

The next best base for hostelry accommodation is Pollença, where the small sanctuary of **Sa Mare de Deu** atop the Puig de Maria offers modest and inexpensive accommodation in spotless rooms with breathtaking views. Several other sanctuaries take in visitors, among them the **Monastery of Cura** (above Randa), the **Sanctuary of Sant Salvador** (near Felanitx) and the **Sanctuary of Monti-Sion** (near Porreres). Finally, don't forget that there is good hostel accommodation atop the **Puig d'Alaró** (Walk 7).

A country code for walkers and motorists

The experienced rambler is used to following a 'country code', but the tourist out for a lark may unwittingly cause damage, harm animals, and even endanger his own life. A country code is especially important on Mallorca, where you often cross private land, and where the rugged terrain can lead to dangerous mistakes.

- **Only light fires** at picnic areas with fireplaces.
- **Do not frighten animals**. The goats and sheep you may encounter on your walks are not tame. By making loud noises or trying to touch or photograph them, you may cause them to run in fear and be hurt.
- **Walk quietly** through all farms and take care not to provoke the dogs. Ignore their barking and keep your walking stick out of their sight — remember, it is only to be shown to an unfriendly, unchained dog.
- **Leave all gates just as you found them**, whether they are at farms or on the mountainside. Although you may not see any animals, the gates do have a purpose — generally to keep goats or sheep in (or out of) an area.
- **Protect all wild and cultivated plants**. Don't try to pick wild flowers or uproot saplings. Obviously fruit and other crops are someone's private property and should not be touched. *Never walk over cultivated land.*
- **Take all your litter away with you.**
- *Do not take risks!* This is the most important point of all. Do not attempt walks beyond your capacity, and do not wander off the paths described if there is any sign of mist or if it is late in the day. **Never walk alone**, and *always* tell a responsible person *exactly* where you are going and when you expect to return. Remember, if you become lost or injure yourself, it may be a long time before you are found. On all long walks, carry a whistle, torch, extra water and warm clothing — as well as some high-energy food, like chocolate.

Organisation of the walks

I hope that the book is set out so that you can plan your walks easily — depending on how far you want to go, your abilities and equipment, and the season. Wherever you are based on the island, there should be a walk within relatively easy reach — and almost all the suggested walks are accessible by public transport.

You might begin by considering the large fold-out touring map between pages 16 and 17. Here you can see at a glance the overall terrain, the road network, and the exact orientation of the walking maps in the text. Quickly flipping through the book, you'll find that there's at least one photograph for every walk.

Having selected one or two potential excursions from the map and the photographs, turn to the relevant walk. At the top of the page you'll find planning information: distance/time, grade, equipment, and how to get there by public or private transport. If the grade and equipment specifications are beyond your scope, don't despair! *There's always at least one short version of each walk,* and in most cases these are far less demanding of agility and equipment.

When you are on your walk, you will find that the text begins with an introduction to the overall landscape and then quickly turns to a detailed description of the route itself. The large-scale maps (all 1:50,000) have been specially annotated and set out facing the walking notes wherever possible. Times are given for reaching certain key checkpoints. Giving times is always tricky, because they depend on so many factors, but my times fall mostly in the range 2-4km per hour, depending on the terrain. Note that these times **include only minimal stops** — to catch your breath or take a photo. Be sure to allow extra time for other breaks — picnicking, swimming, etc.

Many of the **symbols** used on the walking maps are self-explanatory, but here is a key to the most important:

▬▬▬	main road	▮	castle
▬▬▬	secondary road	⊟	*talaia* (see page 60)
══ ─	tarmac lane/track	*P*	picnic (see pages 10-16)
- - - -	footpath	✚	monastery/church
—600—	height in metres	⸙	spring, water tank
3 →	route of the walk and direction	▣	best views
3 →	alternative route	月	picnic tables
🚗	car parking	🚌	bus stop
		🚆	train station

Spanish and Mallorquín

While Spanish is still the official language of Mallorca, most of the islanders speak Mallorquín amongst themselves. The regional autonomy movement has gained much ground on the island since publication of the last edition of this book, and place names are gradually being changed from Spanish to Mallorquín. Since maps and leaflets published by our regional tourist office now refer to villages, streets, and public monuments by their Mallorquín names, I have done the same, recognising that these names will prevail in future. In the rare instance where this might result in confusion, the Mallorquín is followed by the Spanish name.

Language hints for walkers and picnickers

In the tourist centres almost everyone speaks at least a little English. But once out in the countryside, a few words of Spanish will be helpful, especially if you lose your way.

Here's an (almost) foolproof way to communicate in Spanish. First, memorise the few short key questions and their possible answers, given on the next page. Then, when you have your 'mini-speech' memorised, always ask the many questions you can concoct from it **in such a way that you get a 'sí' (yes) or 'no' answer.** *Never* ask an open-ended question like 'Where is the main road?'. You won't understand the answer — especially as it's likely to be given in Mallorquín! Instead, ask the question and then *suggest the most likely answer yourself.* For instance: 'Good day, sir. Please — where is the road to Lluc? Is it straight ahead?'. Now, unless you get a 'sí', try: 'Is It to the left?'. If you go through the list of answers to your own question, you will eventually get a 'sí' response — probably with a vigorous nod of the head — and this is just that

bit more reassuring than relying solely on sign language. A good phrase book is a very valuable aid, in which you will find other 'key' phrases and answers.

Following are three of the most likely situations in which you may have to practice some Spanish. The dots (...) show where you will fill in the name

The St Pere chapel at Escorca, where Walk 11 begins

of your destination. The approximate pronunciation of place names is shown in the index, on pages 140-142.

■ Asking the way

The key questions

English	Spanish	pronounced as
Good day, sir (madam, miss).	Buenos días, señor (señora, señorita).	Boo-**eh**-nohs **dee**-ahs, sen-**yor** (sen-**yor**-ah, sen-yor-**ee**-tah).
Please — where is	Por favor — dónde está	**Poor** fah-**vor** — **dohn**-day es-**tah**
the road to ... ?	la carretera a ... ?	la cah-reh-**teh**-rah ah ... ?
the footpath to ...	la senda de ... ?	lah **sen**-dah day ... ?
the way to... ?	el camino a ... ?	el cah-**mee**-noh ah ... ?
the bus stop?	la parada de autobus?	lah pah-**rah**-dah day ow-toh-**boos**?
Many thanks.	Muchas gracias.	**Moo**-chas **gra**-thee-as.

Secondary question, leading to a yes/no answer

English	Spanish	pronounced as
Is it here?	Está aquí?	Es-**tah** ah-**kee**?
straight ahead?	todo recto?	**toh**-doh **rec**-toh?
behind?	detrás?	day-**tras**?
to the right?	a la derecha?	ah lah day-**reh**-chah?
to the left?	a la izquierda?	ah lah eeth-kee-**er**-dah?
above?	arriba?	ah-**ree**-bah?
below?	abajo?	ah-**bah**-hoh?

■ Making arrangements with a taxi driver

English	Spanish	pronounced as
Please —	Por favor	**Poor** fah-**vor**
take us to ...	llévanos a ...	l-**yay**-vah-nos ah ...
and return	y volver	ee vol-**vair**
for us at ...	para nosotros a ...	**pah**-rah nos-**oh**-tros ah ...

(Instead of memorising hours of the day, simply point out the time when you wish him to return on your watch, and get his agreement.)

■ Meeting a landowner who denies you access

See notes on page 55 about right of way. If you believe that you have right of way, you might ask:

English	Spanish	pronounced as
We are going to ...	Nos vamos a ...	Nos **vah**-mohs ah ...
Please —	Por favor	**Poor** fah-**vor** —
show us	muéstranos	moo-**es**-trah-nohs
the way.	el camino.	el cah-**mee**-noh.
Many thanks.	Muchas gracias.	**Moo**-chas **gra**-thee-as.

■ Once in a while you may meet people who do not speak Spanish. Greet them in Mallorquín and then pronounce *very carefully* the name of the place you are looking for (see Index for pronunciation of landmarks in this book). The Mallorquín for 'Good morning' is *Bon dia* (Bone **dee**-ah); 'Good afternoon' is *Bonas tardas* (**Bone**-ahs **tar**-dahs).

Island customs — past and present

Some of the customs referred to in the book may be unfamiliar to walkers exploring Mallorca for the first time. I hope the following explanations will be of interest.

Caça a coll

Thrushes are considered a great delicacy on Mallorca, and *caça a coll* (**thrush-netting** — or, literally, 'hunting at the saddle') is a long-standing tradition in the Balearics. Thrushes arrive in late autumn and winter from colder countries, and are especially fond of olives, but are themselves prey for larger birds, such as falcons and kestrels. Thus the thrushes fly only at dusk and in the early morning — between the tops of the tall oaks, where they take refuge at night, and the lower olive orchards. They tend to glide *between* the trees and not above them, so as to protect themselves from the keen eyes of the bigger birds of prey. The islanders noticed these habits and long ago devised a method of catching the birds. They thin out linear 'passages' between the trees (see illustration opposite) and span a huge net held on two canes across the end of a passage. The *caçador* waits silently, hidden behind a bush and, when the birds fly down towards the netting, he quickly folds it over, capturing his unfortunate victims.

Many restaurants on Mallorca include this delicacy on their menus — the most popular dish perhaps being *tords amb col,* or roast thrushes in cabbage leaves. It can be quite delicious, if you can force yourself to stop thinking of the poor little creature migrating happily to the sun, only to land up in the cooking pot!

Cases de neu (Spanish: casas de nieve)

The *cases de neu* ('**snow houses**') are deep pits, only found on the highest part of the sierra. Here snow was stored to make ice before the advent of the refrigerator.

There are many of these cases de neu on the mountains of Massanella, Major, Teix and Tomir.

During the winter months, when heavy snow fell on the mountains, a group of men would set out for the peaks and fill these deep, stone-walled holes with snow, packing it down hard. Once full, the pit was covered over with ashes or salt, and it remained frozen solid until the arrival of warmer weather. One man would stay behind, to tend the salt or ash covering, making repairs if necessary.

In summer, and at night, blocks of ice weighing about fifty kilos (100 lbs) were loaded onto mules and taken down into the towns and villages, where they were used not only to make ice-creams and the like, but also for medicinal purposes. The so-called *oli de*

A well-preserved casa de neu *on the northern slopes of Massanella (Walk 13), a few minutes downhill from the* Coll d'es Prat

A bird's-eye view of thrush-netting passages, seen from the Camí de S'Arxiduc above Son Marroig (Walk 5)

neu ('snow-oil'), which was a mixture of ice and olive oil, was used to heal wounds and was reputed to stop bleeding.

Forns de calç (Spanish: hornos de cal)

You'll see the remains of many of these **ovens** *(forns)* around Mallorca. They were used to produce **lime** *(calç)* for whitening the interiors of houses, or to be mixed with fine gravel for use in building.

The work was usually carried out by three men, labouring day and night for anything between nine and fifteen days. A great amount of heat was necessary to produce the reaction, and in these ovens an enormous quantity of wood was burned to obtain the heat required. Normally the thinner logs — which were not suitable for the charcoal industry (see 'Sitjas' on page 60) — were used, and any amount up to two tons could be burnt during one 'cooking'! A normal-sized oven would produce between a hundred and a hundred and fifty tons of burnt lime in one session.

Santuaris (Spanish: monasterios, santuarios), Ermitas

There are many **sanctuaries** on the island. Some of them are even today the homes of hermits who lead a simple and solitary life. They remind us of medieval times, dressed in full-length brown wool habits, with their heads shaven and their long white beards.

Although much early evidence of hermit life has been discovered on Mallorca, Ramon Llull is accepted by the islanders as being the founder of the monastic life. Born a few years after the invasion of Mallorca by Jaime I in 1229, Llull was the son of a Catalan who accompanied the king during the Reconquest. Ramon Llull himself then became the steward of the future king, Jaime II, while still in his teens. Later, he married Blanca de Picany, by whom he had two children. As he grew older, however, he found that his Latin passions could not be satisfied solely by his wife, and he turned to other lovers in search of further pleasure and deeper fulfillment.

At about the age of thirty, he was suddenly convinced of his sins and turned to strict penitence — making pilgrimages to the sanctuaries of Santiago de Compostela and Montserrat. Back on Mallorca, in 1275 he went to Randa, living in a small grotto on the hillside. Later he founded a missionary school in Valldemossa, where oriental languages were taught to friars who would eventually travel in Asia and Africa to convert the followers of Islam. Llull was martyred in North Africa in 1315, stoned to death by Saracens. His remains were brought back to Mallorca by Genovese merchants, and his relics were placed in the Basilica of Sant Françesc in Palma.

A typical day in the life of a hermit starts at 01.00, when he rises for the first prayers of the day. A second call to prayer comes at 06.00, followed by breakfast and manual labour assigned by the superior. After the main meal is eaten at 12.30, the afternoon and evening are spent in prayer, self-examination, meditation and further labour. Lights are out at 21.00, and each hermit retires to his cell where he rests until, at 01.00, the day repeats itself.

The governing superior resides at the Santuari of Sant Salvador near Felanitx (Car tour 5) and is elected every six years by the hermits themselves. Novices begin their trial periods at S'Ermita de Betlem near Artà (Car tour 4).

Of special interest to lovers of the countryside (and walkers in particular) is the opportunity to stay overnight at various monasteries scattered around the island. The simple accommodation is spotless and, owing to their remote position on hilltops, the views are always superb. See also page 53, 'Where to stay'.

Síquies (Spanish: canaletas)

These **'little canals'** ('canaletas'; the Spanish name is more generally used) may still be seen around the island (see opposite and page 63). Made of stone, they carry water from springs down the hillsides to irrigate crops. Today, most of these delightful free-flowing water-courses have been replaced by metal conduits, for reasons of sanitation and to prevent evaporation — a great loss for lovers of the landscape.

The island's most famous watercourse, the Canaleta de Massanella (shown opposite), is 7km long and runs from the Font d'es Prat to Mancor del Valle. Its history is interesting. The work is attributed to a certain Montserrat Fontanet, a Mallorcan pig farmer employed on the Massanella farmholding during the 18th century. The owner of this large property had brought engineers from France, England, Italy and the Spanish mainland, to plan and execute the channelling of waters from the Es Prat spring. All these eminent engineers agreed that such a feat was technically impossible, after which Señor Fontanet offered to do the job himself. His employer agreed to the suggestion, and the work was reportedly completed in two years — a record feat by any standards.

Sitjas (Spanish: círculo de carboneros)

Circular earthen mounds, ringed with stones and now covered in moss — sitjas — are the only remains of the old charcoal industry. In summer months the charcoal-makers lived with their families in the oak woods on the mountainsides. The sturdiest logs from the holm oak were used, and the fires burned round the clock, producing about one and a half tons of charcoal in a week. But the work was poorly paid. Sometimes the remains of a stone hut dwelling are to be found near the sitjas (see photograph on page 62).

Talaias (Spanish: atalayas)

Talaias are **ancient watchtowers**, built in the latter half of the 16th century, to guard against the frequent attacks of pirates and the ever-growing menace of invasion by the Turks.

You can explore the vertiginous Canaleta de Massanella as an optional detour during Walk 13

More than thirty of these *talaias* were in action in the year 1595, and much of the credit for their strategic siting is due to the magnificent work of Juán Binimelis — an astrologer, mathematician, doctor, priest and chronicler. His vast knowledge of Mallorca's terrain, of topography, of artillery and of engineering made it possible to raise these stone outposts at the most suitable points. At the same time, other means of defence — such as Sa Torre in the Port of Alcúdia — were in the planning stages.

From these high points of vigilance (sometimes also called *talaias de foc* or 'fire towers'), approaching sea-craft could be seen at a great distance, and fire and smoke signals were relayed across the island, warning of the danger. Once the enemy was sighted, the coastal inhabitants could take refuge (see notes about the Torre de Canyamel on the next page), while the alerted naval forces would immediately move to the threatened areas.

You will encounter these watchtowers all round the island, and you'll visit several of them if you take any of our island walks. But even if you only see Mallorca from a car or coach, you'll surely visit the Talaia de Ses Animes (photograph below), just south of Banyalbufar, now a superbly-renovated *mirador*.

Let's consider just one interesting example of this network of watchtowers in action: a relay of signals between the Talaia de Albercutx on the Formentor Peninsula (Car tour 3), the Talaia de Alcúdia and the talaia at Penya Rotja on the Cape of Pines (Walk 20) and the Talaia de Morey and the Torre de Aubarca in the Artà mountains (Walk 21; photograph page 133), more than adequately covered the only northern routes of entry to the island — the bays of Pollença and Alcúdia.

If you are fortunate enough to be travelling on a stormy afternoon, and a sunshaft breaks through menacing cloud to fall suddenly on a mountaintop *talaia*, this dramatic moment will stay in your memory long afterwards.

The dramatically-sited Talaia de Ses Animes (Car tour 1) has been refurbished since this photograph was taken. Now a superb mirador, *it overlooks the coast and the terraces at Banyalbufar (see photograph page 21).*

Above: sitja encountered on Walk 5. *Left:* the Torre de Canyamel, built in the 14th century over Arab and Roman foundations. Here people took refuge during pirate sieges, once alerted by flares from a talaia.

Far left: farm with a well (pou) and a furnace for firing tiles in the background. Left: a water-course (síquia or canaleta) at Ternelles, near Pollença. Right: the old houses of Es Cosconar, built into caves, in the valley below Lluc Monastery

Above left: balcony made from an old wine press. Above right: a spring (font) and water tank (safareig) at the Finca de l'Ofre (Walk 9) is home to a duck. Right: sheep crowd us off the trail at Orient (Walk 8).

1 SANT ELM • CALA BASSET • SA TRAPA • PUNTA D'ES FABIOLET • SES BASSES • ANDRATX

Distance/time: 14km/8.7mi; 5h30min

Grade: fairly easy but quite long; ascents/descents totalling about 450m/1475ft and some scrambling over rocks. From Ses Basses wide tracks all the way down to Andratx.

Equipment: hiking boots, water, picnic, sunhat, binoculars; anorak and extra jumpers in winter; swimwear and suncream in summer

How to get there: 🚌 to Sant Elm (Timetable 7). If travelling by 🚗, park in Andratx and take a taxi or bus to Sant Elm to start the walk. *To return:* 🚌 from Andratx (Timetable 5)

Shorter walk: Sant Elm — Cala Basset — Sa Trapa — Sant Elm. 9km/ 5.6mi; 3h20min; grade and equipment as above (ascents of about 350m). 🚌 or 🚗 to/from Sant Elm. Follow the main walk to Sa Trapa (1h40min). To return, keep uphill on the wide track from Sa Trapa, over the mountain pass, then descend to a fork (2h45min), where you turn right for Sant Elm (signposted). *See route 'a' on the map.*

Alternative walk: S'Arracó — Sa Trapa — Punta d'es Fabiolet — Ses Basses — S'Arracó. 13km/8mi; 5h; grade and equipment as main walk (ascents of about 350m). 🚌 to/from S'Arracó (Timetable 7 or *summer only* service running between Sant Elm and S'Arracó every two hours; enquire in advance at a tourist office), or 🚗 to/from S'Arracó (park by the school in the Camí d'es Castellas, where the walk ends). *See walking notes on page 68 and route 'b' on the map.*

Short alternative walk: S'Arracó — Puig Basset — S'Arracó. 4.5km/ 2.8mi; 1h45min; fairly easy ascent of 250m/820ft to Puig Basset — and the view is worth every minute of it! Access/return as Alternative walk; park on the Camí d'es Castellas, or at the cemetery by the KM5 marker. Equipment: stout walking shoes, water, picnic or snack; anorak in winter. *See notes on page 69 and route 'c' on the map.*

About 7km along the winding country road from Andratx, on the westernmost point of the island, lies Sant Elm. A quiet seaside village in winter, a busy little resort in summer, it looks out towards the rocky island of Sa Dragonera across a narrow stretch of deep blue water. There are many lovely woodland walks in this area, but most interesting is the ascent up to the ruins of an ancient Trappist monastery set among almond tree terraces high up on the cliff-tops. The route then continues along rugged red cliffs with magnificent coastal views (one can see as far as Sóller or even further on a clear day), before turning inland across some of the quietest, most uninhabited hills on the island. Finally we descend a green and fertile valley into the town of Andratx (Andraitx in Spanish).

From the bus stop by the windmill (the last stop) in Sant Elm, **begin the walk** along the Avinguda de Sa Trapa. Follow this road towards the woods. The tarmac soon ends, and the way becomes an earthern track. In **15min**

Approaching the Torre de Cala Basset (top); the tower's dramatic location, as seen from the cliffs below Sa Trapa (middle); the northern headlands, from the coastal path beyond the Punta d'es Fabiolet viewpoint (bottom)

you'll reach a house, Ca'n Tomeví. Here the track divides: to the left one can follow a short route up to the watchtower above Cala Basset (Picnic 1b; photograph top right), to the right lies the way to S'Arracó, and although the sign to 'Sa Trapa' points to the right, we follow a path straight ahead, up through the trees. Coming up to another wide track (**20min**), turn left between two stone posts to head down to Cala Basset. It takes about 15 minutes to reach this delightful sheltered little rocky cove where, on a warm day, it is a pleasure to down rucksacks and enjoy a swim before climbing up the cliffs.

Back up on the main track, turn left just beyond the two stone posts (opposite where you came up from Ca'n Tomeví), to follow the ascending path. It soon starts to climb quite steeply, eventually coming up out of the woods onto the rocky cliffs, from where you will have some good views down over the bay of Sant Elm and across to the isle of Dragonera. The path levels out for a short while further up (**1h10min**), climbs the side of another cliff, levels out again, and finally climbs the last rocky slope. Near the top of this last ridge, keep a sharp lookout for the red paint spots indicating a sharp turn right, over some

65

Sa Dragonera, from the viewpoint above the Punta d'es Fabiolet

large boulders — if you miss this you will come to rather a precipitous edge! Once over the brow of the cliff (**1h35min**), you can see the ruins ahead. The path now descends gently to Sa Trapa (**1h40min**).

The old monastery buildings are set back from the cliff-edge on a series of sloping grassy terraces planted with almond trees. Trappist monks lived here until the end of the 18th century, when the Spanish government abolished many of these institutions for both political and financial reasons. Now it is owned by the Balearic Ornithological Group (GOB), who are restoring the main building for use as a refuge for hikers. (One can already spend the night here; telephone 721105 for information.) Walk past the monastery and round past the old millhouse opposite (also restored), and continue to the cliff-edge. Do be careful of the unprotected drop: a young Mallorcan met an untimely death here; you can see the memorial stone placed at the viewpoint by his family. Back at the monastery, you will find plenty of good spots to take elevenses or have an early picnic lunch under the almond trees.

The continuing route starts on the uphill track just behind the monastery. About eight minutes up, take the narrow path off to the left (on the second sharp bend to the right). It climbs gradually through the woods (sadly scarred by a huge forest fire in 1994), then comes out at open cliffs further up. Levelling out, the path winds amongst rocks and comes to a large cairn at a junction (**2h20min**). Turn left here; after a few minutes you will come to the amazing walled-in lookout atop the Punta d'es Fabiolet, with its fantastic 'aerial' views of the isle of Sa Dragonera. *Take* *extra care* at this vertiginous spot, please! Although it is walled-in, the wall is low, and there is a sheer drop to the sea some 400m/1300ft below.

Return to the cairn and now keep left (ie, your back to the sea), to continue along the stony path. Watch where you place your feet but, five minutes further along, lift your eyes from the path, to enjoy a marvellous view along a great stretch of the northwestern coastline — it really is a beautiful sight. You can also see the rounded summit of S'Esclop (Walk 3) dominating the horizon high above the coast — I can already hear the cameras clicking! Now the path begins to descend gradually, and it eventually turns inland. Keep right at the first little clump of trees, and follow the path which soon widens out. Not long after passing an old house up on the left, you come to an abandoned house with a front porch at Ses Basses (**2h45min**). This is also a nice, quiet place to picnic, sitting on the old stone seat in the porch, with the lonely hills and valleys unfolding away into the distance.

After either a picnic or a drink stop, continue down the wide track past the house. The track bends to the right and left. *(On the first straight stretch, the path off to the right, by the cairn, is the return route to S'Arracó for the Alternative walk.)* The track then continues for about another 45 minutes over the solitary hills (keep left at **3h10min**, where the track has descended to the woods). The way then becomes an earthen track, and a pleasantly easy walk through the trees brings you to a large clearing (**3h30min**) just below the KM106 marker on the main Andratx/Estellencs road (C710). People often park here, to walk to Sa Trapa and back.

Walk up to the road, then take the wide track that slopes down to the right immediately, and keep left at the fork just after. You will pass two gates and come onto a tarmac lane 15 minutes later. Keep on this lovely old country lane; it winds downhill through a beautiful sheltered basin which the local people call the 'Silent Valley'. Green and fertile, and lush with all kinds of flowers and vegetation, it is especially idyllic when the area is abloom with pink and white almond blossom in January or early February!

You come into Andratx along the Carrer de Barcelona at **4h50min**. At the end, turn left along the main road. Follow the main road to the end, where it turns down right (below the church), to come to the beginning of the C710 (signposted to Estellencs; **5h10min**). Turn left up this road, to find the bus stop and car park on the right (**5h30min**).

Alternative walk

Walk out of S'Arracó towards Sant Elm on the PM103. When you come to a cemetery on the right (at KM5; **15min**), take the lane at the back of the parking area (signposted 'Sa Trapa'). Keep up the slope for five minutes, then turn right on a rough track. But leave this track almost immediately, to follow a narrow path alongside a wire fence (yellow and blue waymarks). At the corner of the fence, turn left downhill on a wider path. In **25min** go right on a track (red arrow on the tree). After a few minutes descend into the valley on a steepish rocky path (red paint on rocks, by the side of a telegraph pole). Coming down onto a wide track in the valley floor, go right. At **50min** the track divides — left to Sant Elm, right to Sa Trapa. Keep right and, further along, keep left on the main track, ignoring the track off to the right. You head steeply up over a pass and then descend to Sa Trapa (**1h 50min**). Now follow the main walk from the 1h40min-point to the house at Ses Basses. Just beyond it, when you come to the first straight stretch of track after the bends (**2h50min**), turn down sharp right on a narrower track (cairn). Wind down into the trees, then veer left, skirt the side of a valley, and climb the slopes of the Puig de Corso. This is a magnificent part of the walk — silent hills and valleys all around and not a sign of civilisation! At **3h25min**, coming over the brow of the mountain, you have a panoramic view across to where we were walking earlier. The path starts to wind downhill now, becoming narrow and rocky. It passes a stone house, goes through a gap in a stone wall (**3h40min**) and heads towards the woods. A lovely resting place appears on the right at **3h55min** — an open grassy area edged by an unusual natural rock wall. From here the way reverts to track. At **4h20min** take a sharp right U-turn at the fork and keep downhill on the main track until you see a red arrow and paint spot on a tree, where the track bends left. Leave the track here and keep ahead through the trees along a path. Following the paint spots, bear slightly right. Go through a wooden gate and walk between two wire fences, at the end of which you come onto another track (**4h35min**). Turn left and continue along main track; it soon starts to descend and eventually joins a wide dirt road. Turn right and walk down into

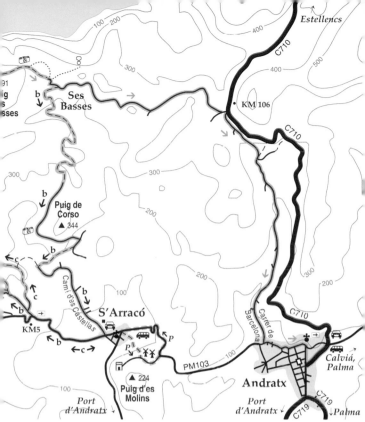

S'Arracó, coming onto the Camí d'es Castellas at **4h55min**. Continue along to the main road and turn up left to the bus stop.

Short alternative walk

Follow the Alternative walk: start up the lane by the cemetery, but cut off right onto a dirt track almost immediately, descending past a little house with solar panels. Then go right again, along a narrow, undulating earthen path. Pass a stone hut (**15min**) and descend to cross a little valley, with a streambed to the right. Go through a field of almond trees, and dip down again, to cross the stream. On the far side, meet a wider path and a stone with red and yellow paint spots (to the right the Alternative walk comes back to S'Arracó). Turn left on the wider path, cross the stream again, and then ascend quite steeply, to a saddle with two large cairns (**40min**). Turn right here and follow the narrow path up to a stone shelter (**1h**). A couple of minutes more up to the left is a fabulous viewpoint perched on the edge of rocky Puig Basset, with splendid panoramic views of Sant Elm, its surrounding mountains and valleys, and the isle of Dragonera. To return, descend for about 10 minutes, then look for a rock at ground level with 'S.T' (San Telmo, the Spanish name for Sant Elm) in red-painted letters; it lies just before the saddle you came up to from the other side. Follow this narrow rocky path, keeping left about five minutes further down. Then skirt the wire fence and rejoin the wide track just above the cemetery (**1h45min**). Turn left for S'Arracó.

69

2 THREE ROUTES UP THE GALATZO MOUNTAIN

Walk a (from Sa Font d'es Pí): 7km/4.3mi; 3h; moderate ascent of 400m/1300ft, requiring stamina (there is a very rocky scree to cross, and some scrambling up high rocks near the summit). Equipment: hiking boots or strong shoes, water, picnic, sunhat; anorak and warm clothing in winter. Access/return: 🚌 to/from the Font d'es Pí above Puigpunyent. Coming into Puigpunyent from Palma, turn left along the road to Galilea. After about 200m turn right on a tarmac lane signposted to 'La Reserva' *(note your km reading here)*. Keep following 'La Reserva' signs uphill until you reach a wide three-way fork, where the entrance to 'La Reserva' descends the middle option: keep right here. Veer left 700m above the fork (red arrow on a rock on a bend) and then go right another 400m up, later passing a small quarry. At 4.9km from when you turned in at the first sign, turn up sharp right for some 300m, to an earthen clearing (sufficient room for three or four cars) by the Font d'es Pí. Walking notes begin on page 71.

Walk b (from Puigpunyent): 14km/8.7mi; 6-7h; not technically difficult, but a strenuous climb of about 750m/2460ft — and long; you need to be really fit to do this version. Note also that just over 5km is on (quiet) tarmac lanes. Equipment as (a) above, but take extra food and water. Access/return: 🚌 to Puigpunyent. Either park at the Son Net restaurant (at the entrance to Puigpunyent when coming from Palma) or park at the 35min-point in the walk (reducing the walking time by about 1h). See walking notes on page 73.

Walk c (from the C710 at Estellencs): 7.5km/4.7mi; 5h; strenuous, with steep ascents totalling some 800m/2625ft. Equipment: hiking boots, plenty of water, picnic, sunhat, suncream, whistle; extra clothing, anorak and woollen hat in winter. Access/return: 🚌 to KM97 on the C710 at Estellencs; park well off the road. (Note: If you

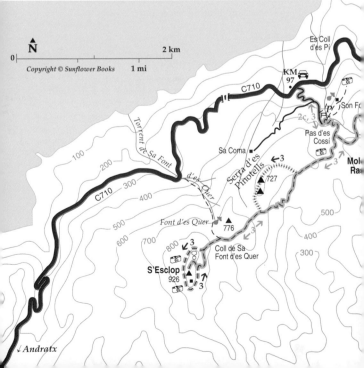

have a 4WD vehicle, there are several good parking areas up the steep track where the walk begins). See walking notes on page 75.

The hike up the rocky Galatzó mountain can be surprisingly easy — or a real challenge. Walk a is decidedly easier than it would appear to be when you look up at this rugged mountain from below. It is considerably less demanding than the ascent of Tomir, and children who are used to hiking will love this mountain adventure! Walk b on the other hand is long and strenuous, with a rocky ascent up to the col, level walking round the ridges (stunning coastal views), and another rocky ascent to the summit — a five-star hike in every sense. Walk c, although not the longest route up Galatzó, is quite strenuous as well. But it offers unsurpassed views all the way up, and brings about a well-deserved feeling of achievement at the end of the day — so if you're bursting with vitality, why not take up the challenge? Whichever version you choose, your reward will be a spectacular panorama down over the western coastline and Palma and, to the northeast, across the mountain peaks that comprise the Serra de Tramuntana, with the fertile plain stretching away below to the south.

Start Walk a by heading up the wide stony track that continues uphill from the Font d'es Pí. At the top, take the narrow path that veers off left, up through the trees (red

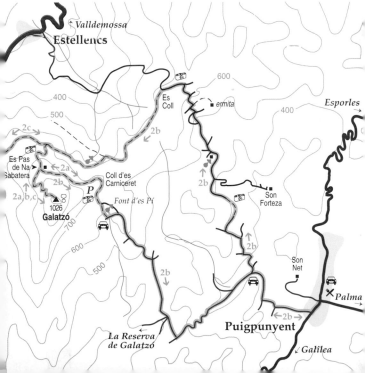

paint marks here). This well-waymarked route winds gently uphill and then rises more sharply, eventually coming out of the trees onto the bare, fire-ravaged slopes below the Coll d'es Carniceret. About **30min** up you will reach the brow of the hill, and what a wonderful surprise will greet you when you glimpse the view over the other side, down over the green slopes of Estellencs, a pretty village caught between the mountains and the coast! Hopefully it is clear — floating mists can often hang around this north side of Galatzó. From this point, you will also be able to see the second stage of our walk — the narrow continuing path to the left: it descends to cross a scree and then rises again, rounding the north face of the mountain and climbing to a second ridge. Follow this, taking extreme care across the scree with its loose rocks (remember not to shout — loud noises can dislodge them). You come up to the ridge, Es Pas de Na Sabatera, at about **1h**; it's a good place to take a break before tackling the third, most strenuous stage of the hike. (The path coming up the other side of the ridge is the ascent route for both Walks b and c).

The final stretch begins from behind the ruins of the old stone refuge here on the ridge. Follow the rocky path, which is fairly steep in places; the way is sporadically marked with red paint, and some cairns. After clambering up some high rocks near the top, veer left and come to the summit at **1h40min**. Unless you are unlucky enough to be caught literally with your head in the clouds, I would say that this is one of the best vantage points from which to contemplate the sierra — a rugged horizon of rocky peaks

Looking north to Galatzó

stretching away into the distance.

Descend the same way; it takes about 1h20min to come back down to the clearing and your parked car at the Font d'es Pí (**3h**).

Start Walk b from the Son Net restaurant car park (or continue by car). Walk up to the STOP sign and turn left on the road signposted to Galilea. After about 200m turn right (signposted 'La Reserva'). Now follow 'La Reserva' signs for about 1.4km, when you will come to a widening in the road, where there are some rubbish containers on the left (**25min**; motorists can park here, well tucked in).

Here we take a sharp right U-turn down the lane; at the next fork, head up to the left. This wide tarmac lane winds up the hillside between chalets and little houses (keep right at a first fork, left a few minutes later, and then right again). On this last bend, a cacophony of barking dogs will accompany you to the top! The tarmac ends (**55min**), and we continue up some rough steps cut into the earth, to the right. Keeping alongside the wire fence, we come to a stone wall with built-in steps and a wooden ladder. On the other side, veer slightly left along the narrow path, which soon levels out and widens. Here there is a good view down right through the trees over a beautiful example of a 16th-century Mallorcan aristocratic mansion, Son Forteza. Elevated on terraces above Puigpunyent and surrounded by orange and lemon groves, its romantic landscaped gardens boast an impressive waterfall approached by a pergola of 76 columns and a natural lake (not visible from here). Don Felipe Villalonga i Fuster de Puigdorfila, a direct descendent of a Spanish noble, still lives there. At the fork, keep down to the right, and at **1h10min** join the main route that comes up from Son Forteza.

Now turn up left and continue along the main track, through this very peaceful and picturesque landscape of open terraces, passing a freshwater spring. At **1h25min**, just after a sharp bend to the left, take the track up to the right (the continuing track leads to an abandoned house). Go right again just before a gap in the stone wall; from here onwards there are some cairns and red paint waymarking. Soon go through a gateway. At the next fork (**1h30min**) keep up to the left and then continue straight ahead, at **1h37min** going through a gate (please close it behind you).

73

Now turn right; you will see a red arrow on the wall opposite. Walk alongside a stone wall, soon coming up to a wide track. Cross it and follow the red paint marks up through the woods. When you come up to another wide track, follow it uphill to the right. You will pass by a gap in the stone wall (**1h50min**); it is the entrance to an old *ermita,* and you can see the abandoned building sitting on the terraces if you look over the wall a little further uphill. On the Sunday after Easter, all the villagers from Puigpunyent come up to this *ermita* for a picnic, on the so-called 'Day of the Angels'. Keep up left at the next fork, and then continue straight ahead, always following the red paint spots and cairns.

At **2h10min** turn up sharp left (red spot on a tree trunk); another few minutes will bring us up to a level stretch, where the route, now less rocky, becomes a pleasant earthen track through the silent oak woods. You may like to look at one or two old stone woodcutters' dwellings hiding in the trees along here, to the left and right. Climb the wooden ladder over the dividing wall of Es Coll (**2h20min**), and immediately, if it is clear, you will see the little village of Estellencs nestling at the foot of the mountains far below you, and enjoy a superb outlook over a stretch of the rugged northwestern coastline. Time for a photo or three!

Continue on down the easy, wide track to the left for about 200m; then, on a bend, *look carefully* for the faint earthen path going off left through the trees (some cairns here). This is our route, and we will now follow this narrow path through the trees for about half an hour, rounding the contours of these high wooded slopes, with excellent coastal views and some stunning views of our friend the Galatzó mountain — from this viewpoint it look invincible — like a smaller version of the Matterhorn! Some 20 minutes along, a sheltered rocky clearing to the right of the path makes a good picnic spot, with large stone slabs useful as a 'table' — but note that there is also an excellent picnic area in a clearing 15 minutes further up. At **2h55min** go through a gap in an old stone wall, after which the path descends a little gulley.

A couple of minutes later, just where the path begins to ascend again, look very carefully for the beginning of our somewhat arduous ascent to the peak — it's a camouflaged little earthen path that goes up to the left (some small cairns here). Climbing through rough scrubs, this fairly overgrown path becomes steeper and stonier, and rises for

about 10 minutes (keep to the right of the trees bordering the crest, with Galatzó straight ahead of you). You will come up to a level stretch, where there is a clearing (**3h10min**); this is my favourite picnic place on the hike. It's very tempting to take a *siesta* after eating, but there's quite a steep climb ahead, so better continue!

To leave the clearing, veer right, behind the bushes, and follow the path which winds through the trees and goes through a gap in another stone wall, after which it crosses a *sitja*. Now we start to climb in earnest, and eventually come up to a signposted mountain crossroads at **3h45min**. Here another path comes in through a rocky pass to the right (this is the ascent route of Walk c and also leads to the magnificent S'Esclop mountain which we visit in Walk 3). Our onward route to the Galatzó peak makes a U-turn up to the left here, rising above our incoming trail. As you climb higher, take a breather to admire the absolutely spectacular scenery all around; it is truly breathtaking! Twenty minutes more will bring us to a second mountain pass, the Pas de Na Sabatera; the little stone refuge here is now a ruined heap of rubble, but there is room to sit and recuperate some energy for the final assault (described in Walk a on page 72: see notes from the 1h-point). We come up to the summit at **4h35min**.

To return to Puigpunyent, come back down to the stone hut ruins, and turn right, following the narrow descending path and crossing the scree *with care*. You will rise to the next ridge at **5h15min**. Then take the path down the opposite side, towards the bare hill with a stone wall across it. You will eventually come down to the woods and, further down, onto the wide stony lane which leads to the Font d'es Pí spring (where Walk a begins and ends; **5h 35min**). From here, keep left and, on coming down to the tarmac road ten minutes later, go left again. Now you have a 5km-long walk along a (quiet) tarmac lane, and you will soon pass a small quarry. At the next junction go straight ahead. At the following junction, keep left again, passing the entrance to La Reserva on your right. Winding down-hill, you will arrive back at your parked car at **6h10min** — or at **6h30min**, if you parked at the Son Net restaurant.

Walk c begins at KM97 on the C710; a large sign ('Son Fortuny') a minute up the wide track indicates the beginning of the route. Follow the notes for Walk 3 on page 77 as far as the Pas d'es Cossí at the **45min** point. Then turn left to continue on a less demanding path that ascends much more gently, just below the flat-topped rocky elevation known as the 'Moleta Rasa' (the 'flat-topped elevation'). We cross a torrent depression by a stone well and, soon after, a very impressive view of the huge rocky massif of S'Esclop (photograph below) fills the south-western horizon.

Once over the ridge, S'Esclop disappears and we are confronted with her neighbour, the enormous jagged triangular peak of Galatzó — today's destination. Our trail now crosses a small prairie dotted with spiky pampas grass and rosemary scrubs, some sporadic clumps of pine woods here and there, and far-reaching views to the sloping pine-covered Puntals mountain (896m/2940ft) towering above Estellencs to the left. Further on, a shady clump of trees by some large rocks makes a pleasant picnic spot.

Continue along the trail; it descends slightly before starting to rise again through the trees, and soon becomes a narrow rocky path. At **1h35min** it comes up onto the tail-end of a level stretch of stony path, by the side of a small solitary pine. Here we turn left, to come up a few minutes later to a signposted mountain crossroads (**1h40min**). Walk b joins us here: now follow the notes for Walk b from the 3h45min-point (page 75), up to the peak (**2h30min-3h**) where, somewhat breathless, but loving every minute, you your efforts will be repaid in full!

Descend via the same route (**5h**).

3 S'ESCLOP

Distance/time: 10km/6.2mi; 6-7h

Grade: moderate, with a climb and descent of about 650m/2130ft. Only recommended for the intrepid trail-finder, however: the path is somewhat difficult to distinguish at times, although there are cairns. The summit is rough and surrounded by a rocky wilderness, and should not be climbed by the inexperienced. Not recommended in changeable weather conditions.

Equipment: hiking boots, water, picnic, compass, whistle, suncream and sunhat, extra rations; anorak and warm clothing in winter

How to get there and return: 🚌 to KM97 on the C710 at Estellencs. Park by the main road, well tucked in. (Note: Those with 4WD vehicles can park up the beginning of the steep track followed in the walk.)

The 'lost world' of S'Esclop is a wonderful adventure! However, it is not for the inexperienced; the extensive stretch between the Galatzó and S'Esclop mountains is a wilderness of rocks, rough scrubs and high pampas grass, an impressive but lonely landscape, with but a few goat trails, and hardly any shelter in a storm. Yet the panoramic views from the summit surpass all expectations! So, if you're a hardy hiker and love adventure, join me in this challenge — I guarantee a superb day's walking!

Start the walk on the steep wide track that begins at KM97 on the Andratx/Estellencs road (C710). At **15min** turn left at a fork, as indicated by a wooden sign. The track levels out, then dips and rises through the woods, and

winds up left to a picnic site (**25min**). Ignore the track ahead through the gateway here (signposted to Ses Serveres); go right, to walk up through the picnic area. You will pass a typical woodcutters' dwelling complete with thatched roof, and come to a wide trail signposted 'Galatzó — Pas d'es Cossí'. Follow this path sharp right uphill. It soon becomes a narrow rocky path, winding up steeply between two reddish escarpments.

At **45min** we come up to the Pas d'es Cossí, and another wooden signpost: 'Galatzó' is to the left (the route of Walk 2c); 'S'Esclop', to-day's destination, is to the right. We now climb a narrow trail marked

Approaching S'Esclop

with some yellow paint spots — essential for route finding here, as various little paths head uphill. Come up to a rocky cairn at **55min**; it marks the top of the ridge. Opposite the cairn, 'Pas d'es Cossí' and 'S'Esclop' are written in faint yellow paint on the rock — not easily seen at first. *(Note: this landmark is easily missed on the way back; you might like to leave something additional here as a marker.)*

Now *carefully* follow the cairn-marked way across this lovely open plain (at times it's hard to spot some of the cairns hiding among the rocks and tall clumps of pampas grass). To the left you can now see the long high western slopes of Galatzó — very impressive from here, and about 15 minutes later the plains of Calvià appear across the valley to the south. The scenery is beautiful, and the silence of this wild and rocky basin between the two south-westernmost summits of the Tramuntana sierra is broken only by the cry of a bird, or the echo of a bleating goat.

At **1h25min** the route approaches a few sparse trees, where the rocky path veers south downhill.* The path takes us towards the right, and then descends into a gulley, amongst some trees. You really have to look hard for the cairns now, to follow the rocky trail as it rises slightly from the gulley and then descends to the right around the head of a valley, among incredibly tall clumps of pampas grass and spiky scrubs. Now a steepish zigzag ascent up a rough overgrown path, waymarked with yellow paint spots, will bring us up to a fairly level area (**2h15min**), where the cairns are well placed and easier to follow. The path becomes earthen and, on the right, there is a barbed wire fence (this is where you will join the main route if you went up over the ridge as described in the footnote).

Now we find ourselves on a little prairie, so pretty in spring, when masses of wild flowers exhibit their bright colours. The path veers left, up through a few trees, and eventually comes up to a saddle, the Coll de Sa Font d'es Quer (**2h45min**). A large circular area is crossed — a good place to picnic, with the huge rocky massif of S'Esclop

*It is possible to leave the main path here (by a fairly large cairn), and instead of going south on the main route, find a way cross-country up the rocky slope to the right (west). You would rise up to a ridge, the Serra d'es Pinotells. Keep left along the tops of this sierra, passing two triangulation points, and then head down a steepish slope alongside a barbed wire fence. You rejoin the main route at the bottom, by a cairn, and turn right to continue (see main walk notes after the 2h15min-point). This route, through scrub, is rough but not difficult, and it is slightly shorter. Note, however, that it is *not waymarked* except for a couple of cairns near the double 'summit' of the ridge.

rising high ahead of us. From this point it is easy to follow the narrow path as it snakes towards the mountain. Just over the col, and looking down to the left, you can see the ruins of an old stone dwelling. Some 10 minutes along ignore a path forking down to the right (it leads to the Font d'es Quer, a mountain spring inside an old mine, and then makes a steep descent through the cleft of the Quer torrent down onto the C710). Since our aim today is the great *mola* of S'Esclop, keep ahead at this point — making for an old stone wall that rises up the slope of the mountain.

Here you can take your pick: you can either round the mountain or follow the main walk up to the summit.

To round the mountain, take the narrow path sloping down to the right (some 100m before a metal sign up on the stone wall). This path completely rounds the northwest slope of S'Esclop just below the rocky summit, with stunning panoramic views down over the westernmost part of the island. This route takes about an hour; the path is not easy to distinguish, but small cairns mark the way. You come up to the far western slope and round the end of the *mola.* From here there are no paths, but the long rocky southern slope can be descended without much difficulty. Then bear left back down towards the path above the ruined hut, completing the circuit of S'Esclop in about 1h30min.

To climb to the summit, keep left along vaguely-trodden goat tracks, following sporadic cairns which will lead you along the only really viable route up the steep rocky cliff. You come up to the summit ridge at **3h50min**. *Here you must leave some kind of marker to help you find the beginning of your descent,* as it can be hard to locate on the way back. Another few minutes towards the left will bring you to the top (926m/3037ft). Just beyond the summit are the ruins of a stone shelter where François Aragó, a Frenchman, lived a solitary existence at the beginning of the 1800s while working on a triangulation point to measure the meridian. If visibility is good, you'll want to remain up here, taking in all the marvellous panoramas that surround you. It is spectacular atop this long and lonely rocky ridge, surrounded by a deserted wilderness, with 'civilisation' stretching out far below you.

Return now to the point of descent and come back down to the Coll de Sa Font d'es Quer. From here, follow the same route back to your car, taking note of your marker to descend to the picnic site. You reach the C710 at KM97 after a tiring but exciting day's hike of about **6-7h**.

4 TWO WALKS FROM SANTA EUGENIA

Walk a (Santa Eugènia — Ses Coves — Puig d'en Marron — Santa Eugènia): 7.5km/4.7mi; 3h; easy, with gentle ascents of under 180m/600ft. Equipment: stout walking shoes, sunhat, picnic, water, insect repellent; anorak in cold weather. Access/return: 🚇 to/from Santa Eugènia. Coming from Palma on the PM304, turn into the second road on the right (by Bar Ca'n Topa) and then take the first left: there is plenty of good parking in the shade on this wide road. Or by 🚌 (Timetable 2); ask to be put off at 'Ses Coves'. The return bus leaves Santa Eugènia from the stop on the corner of Carrer S'Estació. Note: The only convenient buses are on Sundays and holidays.

Short walk a (Puig de Santa Eugènia): 4.5km/2.8mi; 1h30min; easy. Equipment/access as Walk a. Follow Walk a as far as the gates to the Puig d'en Marron (45min) and then pick up the notes at the 2h10min-point. This avoids the ascent up the Puig d'en Marron, but still takes in the wonderful panoramic views from the cross monument.

Walk b (Santa Eugènia — So Na Rossa — Sencelles): 7km/4.3mi; 1h40min; easy, almost level — a good walk for beginners. Equipment: good walking shoes, sunhat, water, picnic (optional); anorak in cold weather. Access: 🚌 to Santa Eugènia (see Walk a above; Sundays and holidays *only*) or bus to Sencelles (Timetable 2) and taxi to Santa Eugènia; return by 🚌 from Sencelles (Timetable 2).

Short walk b (Santa Eugènia — So Na Rossa — Santa Eugènia): 6km/3.7mi; 1h20min; easy. Equipment as Walk b. Access: 🚇 to Santa Eugènia; park by the orchard as described on page 82 ('To start Walk b'). Follow Walk b to So Na Rossa and return the same way.

Walk a is a delightful country walk, beautiful at any time of year. The Puig d'en Marron is draped in a thick blanket of evergreen pine forests, and the hills are riddled with caves containing silent memories of an Arabic past. Walk b is also a very pretty country walk — especially in spring (it is too exposed for a hot summer's day, but viable most of the year). While it is ideal for beginners, I would recommended it to anyone. It winds gently up and down along a ridge, with wonderful vistas across to the Tramuntana mountain range. Just past the old hamlet of So Na Rossa, the view down over the small village of Biniali below the ridge is extremely picturesque.

To start Walk a, walk back to the main road (PM304) from your parked car, and turn left to walk out of the village as far as the turning up left signposted 'Ses Coves' (**20min**). (Start the walk here if you come by bus, deducting 20min from the following times.) Now turn up this pretty country lane, following it round to the left a few minutes later, to come to the picturesque old stone houses of Ses Coves at **30min**, privileged with far-reaching views across the plain. Keep straight ahead where the lane winds down away from the houses, passing a cave on the left with an old wine-press in it (photograph page 12). A wooden door just below

80

The plain from the Puig de Santa Eugènia

it (now overgrown and jammed shut), opens into a huge cool cave where wine vats were once stored.

The lane twists to the right, widens by an old well, and narrows again. On coming to a fork (**40min**), go left through a little valley, dotted with cottages amidst orange groves and flowering fields. You will reach the gated entrance to the Puig d'en Marron at **45min**. This is usually locked, but it is easy to go over the low wall to the left, and so our gentle climb to the top now begins. In spring the beautiful song of the nightingale can be heard echoing in the pine-scented silence; you may spot a variety of other birds and see little rabbits scurrying away into the bushes as your footsteps disturb their peace. Looking to the right after the first bend in the track, you can see other caves on the soft sandstone hillside across the valley.

At **1h05min** the route divides into two earthen tracks. The continuing one goes through the woods between weekend cottages and descends the hill on the south side, to the Camí de Ses Olleries, where you could turn left back to Santa Eugènia. But we take the right-hand turn, to follow the main track. Keep right at each fork, for about another 15 minutes, after which you will leave the woods and come out onto the open grassy plateau which covers the wide brow of the hill. From here, a good deal of the island may be seen. Bear left across the open fields towards the triangulation point (320m/1050ft; **1h25min**), a good place to picnic and admire the views. For explorers: a few minutes further along, the narrow path comes to a wide clearing with a low stone wall to the right, from where the runways of Palma airport are visible. If you are fit enough to climb over the wall, you could follow a narrow path to the right and then left, down to an ancient abandoned hermitage where monks lived from the 1600s up to the 1820s. There are still orange groves in its walled-in gardens … together with an old well and three wooden crosses by the entrance to a cave.

To return, retrace your steps back down the mountain, as far as the gated entrance to the *puig*. Back in the valley (**2h10min**), turn sharp right (the opposite direction from which you came), to continue along the lane. Set back above us on the hillside, a huge mound of large rocks and boulders covered in prickly-pear cacti indicates the site of an ancient Moorish burial ground. Continue up the slope and, after about 150m/yds, where the lane divides, go left downhill, passing the gated, arched entrance to an old well. Take the first turning left beyond this, up to the side of a small house where you should see a red dot on the wall. A narrow path up the hill begins here, through a gap in the stone wall. It takes us up to a rocky pass 10 minutes later. Just below the pass there is a small grassy platform: look behind you for a minute here, to admire the view southwards.

Climb up through the pass — I call it the 'Shangri-La Pass', because it comes up from this lovely little valley, and once through it, the peace and the stillness is left behind, and winds whipping across the plain catch at your clothing! Now climb the low stone wall to the left, to make your way up to the cross monument atop the Puig de Santa Eugènia (245m/804ft; **2h30min**; photograph page 12). What a magnificent view! The extensive Tramuntana sierra stretches across a wide horizon, with the plain below and many towns and villages dotted about like a multicoloured patchwork quilt.

To end the walk, go back down over the stone wall, and head down left past a gnarled old pine, through scrub, to a walled-in stony track. At the bottom, turn right and then left, down the steep rough tarmac. You come into Santa Eugènia's main square at **3h**. Head straight downhill and take the second right to find your car.

To start Walk b, go out of Santa Eugènia towards Algaida along the main road (Carrer S'Aljub). At the end of the village turn left into a lane, opposite an orchard and a sign to Ca'n Puceta. (Some electricity lines cross the road near here.) If you have come by car (Short walk), drive this far and turn right, to park well tucked in by the orchard fence.

Now it's really easy! No left or right turns any more, just follow

the lane all the way to Sencelles. Soon after starting out, you'll see some picturesque windmills on the low hill to your left and, as the hill begins to fall away, the distant mountain range on a blue horizon comes into view. Hopefully the weather is still and clear. Keep straight ahead at a crossroads (**25min**); you are now well into the country-side, surrounded by open fields dotted with small cottages, and bordered on both sides by blackberry bushes, wild asparagus shrubs spiking out of the stone walls and — if it's spring — a multitude of wild gladioli, poppies, daisies and the beautiful blue flowers of the borage plants. Come to the ancient hamlet of So Na Rossa at **40min**, where it seems time has stood still for centuries; grass grows outside the front doors, and the tinkling of sheep bells carries on the breeze. (The walk can be extended here, if you have time to spare, by taking the lane on the right for about another half hour and returning to this point.)

To continue to Sencelles, keep ahead. When the lane bends to the right (**50min**) and another narrower lane leads down left to Biniali, you enjoy a splendid view down over the plain and across to the mountains. Continue following the lane along the ridge, passing wooded areas and open countryside, small pretty cottages and bigger Mallorcan manor houses. Eventually coming out onto the Sencelles/Algaida road, turn left for Sencelles. At the junction, cross over carefully and keep straight ahead until you reach the village square (**1h40min**), where you can find refreshments at the bar while waiting for your bus.

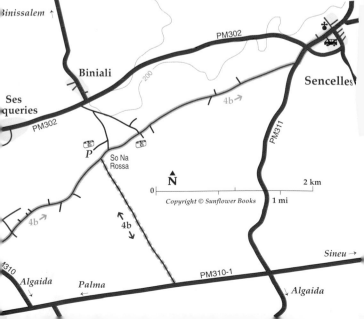

5 VALLDEMOSSA • MIRADOR DE SES PUNTES • CAMI DE S'ARXIDUC • PUIG D'ES TEIX • COMA D'ES CAIRATS • VALLDEMOSSA

See also photo page 22 **Distance/time:** 14km/8.7mi; 6h30min

Grade: strenuous, with ascents totalling some 800m/2625ft. *The high, mist-prone trail of the Camí de S'Arxiduc is only suitable for experienced walkers or good walkers who do not suffer vertigo, and only in good weather conditions (not recommended in high winds).*

Equipment: hiking boots, sunhat, water, picnic, whistle, compass, extra rations; anorak and extra clothing in winter

How to get there and return: 🚐 to/from Valldemossa (Timetable 8), or 🚗 (two large car parks on your right, opposite the main entrance to the village, when coming from Palma)

Short walks: both are strenuous; equipment/access as above

1 Valldemossa — Mirador de Ses Puntes — Coll de S'Estret de Son Gallard — Valldemossa. 7km/4.3mi; 3h30min; a climb and descent of about 450m/1475ft. Follow the main walk to the 2h15min-point, then turn down right, back to Es Pouet. From here go left to retrace your steps to Valldemossa.

2 Valldemossa — SEFOBASA shelter below the Teix — Valldemossa. 6km/3.7mi; 2h30min; a climb and descent of about 350m/1150ft. Follow the main walk up to the house of Son Gual, and walk to the right of the house, through a residential area. Turn left on a wide jeep track 15 minutes later (signposted 'Refugi' further up) and follow it past the Font d'es Polls to the shelter. This walk can be extended to include the climb to the Teix peak (add another 300m/1000ft; 2h).

Alternative walk: Valldemossa — Fontanelles — Camí de S'Arxiduc — Es Teix — Coma d'es Cairats — Valldemossa. 11.5km/7.1mi; 5h; grade/equipment/access as main walk. Follow the main walk to the 1h-point and go through the gateway in the stone wall. Now turn sharp right, to follow the trail up to a fabulous viewpoint on the right over Valldemossa (some 20min up, not long after a bend to the left). Continue ahead; you join the main walk in 2h, by a clump of pines (this area is called 'Fontanelles'). Turn right to follow the main walk from just after the 2h50min-point. (Or turn left to follow the 'Camí' in reverse as far as the Coll de S'Estret de Son Gallard, or the Mirador de ses Puntes, and then back down to Valldemossa — see map.)

O ne of the island's best walks, boasting both splendid views and historical interest. Moreover, it offers so many permutations that anyone with energy can tackle a suitable part of the walk. The main route climbs the thickly pine-wooded mountains near Valldemossa to a fabulous viewpoint, skirts the edge of a high plateau on the Camí de S'Arxiduc, scrambles up to the Teix peak, and then returns to Valldemossa through the pretty Cairats valley.

Start the walk from the bus stop or car park in Valldemossa: walk back up the main road towards Palma, making for the large old house with a square tower (Son Gual) up above the road on the left. Go left up the first road, and then right, coming to the front of Son Gual. *(Here Short*

walk 2 goes straight ahead past the house.) Now go left again, and then right, coming up to a high stone wall. Turn left here, and then curve round to the right, to find a stony track at the top of the rise leading off into the gorse scrubs. Follow it uphill towards a group of lovely umbrella pines, but turn up left just before the pines, climbing a stony path (waymarked). Keep uphill for about five minutes, using the wooden step-ladder to go over the gate, and passing by one or two woodcutters' trails to the right. Then look *carefully* for a little red arrow on a rock at ground level, indicating a sharp turn to the right. Now follow this wide stony woodcutters' trail as it zigzags up through the woods, coming up to a stone wall (**1h**). Go through the gateway.

Walking the Camí de S'Arxiduc, at the edge of the high plateau

(Turn sharp right now, if you are doing the Alternative walk.) Just beyond the gateway you come onto level ground — an extensive shaded area, perfect for taking a breather. From here keep straight ahead through the trees (where vague paths fork off to the right), cross a *sitja*, and come to a wide clearing with an old well — Es Pouet ('little well'

in Mallorcan, but the water is not drinkable). Here there are paths going off at various angles. If you wish to shorten the walk by omitting the ascent to the Mirador de Ses Puntes, take the path off right here: it leads directly up to the Coll de S'Estret de Son Gallard and from there up onto the plateau. The main route keeps straight ahead (north), and then veers left, to wind up the wooded slopes to the Mirador de Ses Puntes (**1h25min**), from where there are superb views down over the coast — if swirling mists don't tease you. *Take extra care here;* parts of the surrounding wall have crumbled away.

Returning from the *mirador,* keep left at the little fork (which you probably didn't even notice on the way up). This is the start of the famous Camí de S'Arxiduc, a mountain bridleway straddling the tops of these peaks and bordering the high plateau, built for the Archduke Luis Salvador of Austria's personal pleasure. The path (faint at times) ascends gradually and climbs a rocky slope up to a trig point (856m; **1h45min**). It then continues through the woods, where lichen-covered branches testify to frequent mists. At **1h55min** we arrive at the ruins of a stone shelter atop a rocky peak (867m) and enjoy our first view down over Sa Foradada, the rock pierced with a hole jutting into the sea below Son Marroig, the archduke's main mansion.

Go carefully down the rocky slope now, and keep on the descending path through the trees, to come to the Coll de S'Estret de Son Gallard (**2h15min**), a mountain cross-roads. A path off right here leads back to Es Pouet, and on the left a path (closed to walkers and not shown on the map) leads down onto the C710. Our route lies straight ahead. Beyond a rest area with stone seats, the rocky path becomes steeper and, after going through a gap in an old stone wall, comes up through the last of the trees to join a stone-laid trail; here turn left, to zigzag up onto the high plateau. Once at the top, you can see forever! To the west, Galatzó (Walk 2) thrusts its peak through scudding clouds, and the high pine-covered mountains of Planici rise up from the valley; below us lies Sa Foradada on a long stretch of rugged coastline; to the south, Palma's huge round bay glistens like a mirror, bordered by the high cliffs of Cap Blanc (Walk 22), with the isle of Cabrera on a hazy horizon; to the northeast the impressive peaks of the Puig Major and Massanella (Walk 14) close off a mountainous panorama. But this stone-laid trail skirts the edge of a high plateau, with very precipitous drops to the left; be *extra vigilant* along here if it happens to be misty or windy!

At about **2h50min** a cairn to the left of the trail marks the beginning of a steep way down the Cingles de Son Rullán onto the C710 just above Son Marroig, and five minutes later we come to the Puig Caragolí (944m/3096ft), a rocky elevation rising off the plateau. An engraved stone plaque dated 1990, homage from all mountaineers to the archduke, can be seen at the top. This makes an excellent picnic spot. A few minutes further along, a small group of pines provides welcome shelter on a hot day. This area is known as Fontanelles. *(The Alternative walk rejoins the main route here.)* Now the path becomes earthen and veers left, to come to another, larger group of pines, also a good picnic spot if Caragolí was too hot — especially if you go off the path to the right to find a cave and water-hole.

Back on the main route, we wind up over another rocky rise and along to a viewpoint over Deià, then turn right to curl down round the head of the valley. Here, on the wide bend (just before the trails begins to descend), you will come to the signposted turn-off to Es Teix. It takes an hour to scramble up to the peak (1064m/3490ft), for more never-to-be-forgotten views, and return to this point.

Rejoining the main route, we now descend into the beautiful Cairats valley, passing by the remains of a *casa de neu* (snow pit). Shortly after, we join a wide track and come to the SEFOBASA hikers' shelter (**5h30min**). Behind it is a covered open area, with a fireplace and stone seats. A little further down the steep track, we pass the picnic area of Sa Font d'es Polls, a mountain spring surrounded by poplars. From here, a rough path leads off left up onto the Serra d'es Cairats (signposted), from where it is possible for the toughest mountain walkers to climb the Teix peak. From here onwards, several of the now-extinct Mallorcan industries (see pages 58-63) can be visited. At **6h** go through a gateway and keep straight ahead, going through a second gateway further on. Where the track ends, fork right onto the tarmac and a little later curve down left to Son Gual, to return to the bus stop/car park (**6h30min**).

See map pages 86-87; see also photographs pages 24, 27

Distance/time: 12km/7.4mi; 4h30min

Grade: quite easy, but fairly long. Possibility of vertigo beyond Deià Cove. Climb of about 300m/1000ft halfway through the walk. Note that swimming is only recommended on calm days.

Equipment: stout shoes, plastic shoes (if swimming), water, picnic, sunhat; swimwear in summer; warm clothing and anorak in winter

How to get there: 🚌 to Deià (Timetable 8)

To return: 🚌 (Timetables 8, 9) or 🚂 from Sóller (Timetable 11)

Short walks

1 Deià — Cala de Deià — Lluc-Alcari — Deià. 6km/3.8mi; 3h; easy. A good walk for beginners, but there is a danger of vertigo where the path nears the edge of the cliffs beyond Deià Cove. Equipment/access as main walk, or by 🚗 to/from Deià. Follow the main walk to Lluc-Alcari and return the same way. *You could make this walk even shorter:* either just walk down to Deià Cove and return the same way (1h10min), or walk back up the tarmac road to the KM61.2 marker on the east side of Deià and catch a bus there (1h15min), or follow the main road back to your car (1h50min). *Alternatively,* if you have a car, drive down to Cala de Deià (from KM61.2) and walk along the coastal path to Lluc-Alcari and back (4km/2h).

2 Deià (Ca'n Puigserver) — Sóller. 8km/5mi; 2h35min; easy, after an initial ascent of some 180m/590ft. Equipment as main walk (less swimwear). Access/return as main walk: get off the bus or park east of Deià, near Ca'n Puigserver (the KM60.2 marker on the C710). You can take a bus back to your car (Timetable 8). Follow the main walk from the 1h55min-point. *You can make this walk even shorter:* follow the main walk from the 1h55min-point to just past Son Coll hamlet, and go left at the bottom of the wide stone steps to find the mountain spring; return same way (4.5km/2.8mi; 1h30min).

The combination of cliff-top paths and mountain air makes this hike irresistible. After sampling the panoramic sea views, the fresh mountain air, and the splendid descent into Sóller, I'm sure you will want to discover more of Mallorca on foot. In the first part of the walk, most of the pathway leads through pine-shaded areas. You can take a dip in the clear blue waters at Cala de Deià itself or at various points where stone steps along this rocky and abrupt but beautiful coastline lead down to the sea. The second half of the walk follows a picturesque route through the mountains down into the pretty Sóller valley. But if you do not feel up to tackling this fairly long hike ... or if you are wondering what to do with a day that 'turned out fine after all' ... either of the short walks (or their even shorter variations) would be ideal.

Start the walk at KM63.1 on the C710, just west of Deià. Go down a wide tarmac lane, turning sharp left in **3min**. When the tarmac ends keep straight ahead: take stone steps past the side of a house (you'll see a sign here, 'To the beach. A la Cala'. The deep bed of the Torrent d'es Salt is on your right. Climb a stile at **10min** and, a couple of minutes further down, bear right — where 'Cala' is painted in white at ground level. Climb a second stile at **15min**, then follow a beautiful stone-laid path. At **20min** join a tarmac road and turn down left, to a wide parking area.

At **30min** come to the pebbly, picturesque little beach at Deià Cove (Cala de Deià), where you will also find a restaurant perched above on the rocks, and a terrace where you can sip something refreshing (if you have come in the summer). You can end Short walk 1 here, to spend time swimming in the lazy waters, while you anticipate a freshly-caught fish dish... or continue towards Lluc-Alcari.

Returning from the cove, take the *second* set of stone steps on your left, up the side of the cliff. At **35min** take the steep earthen path which goes down left, edged by a wooden fence (a good spot from which to photograph Deià Cove). At the bottom, a few metres before a little house, turn up right, and come up a terrace or two to find the coastal path. A little further on, the path becomes well marked with red paint spots, and continues along the coast — at times very near the edge of the cliffs! There is some danger of vertigo at **40min** and beyond.

You will come to some stone steps leading down to the

Deià

water at a point where the path crosses some fallen rocks. *Extra care* is needed here, as the path slopes directly down to the sea! Do *not* cross the stile at **55min** (where the path has caved in), but go round to the right of the big pine tree. Just below here, you will find an excellent place to swim (on calm days) from a stone platform. (The rocks here are full of sea urchins, hence my suggestion of plastic shoes!)

The path continues up through a beautiful wide grassy terrace complete with stone table and seats for picnicking, then narrows again, veering right, round the rocky cliff-edge. Climb two stiles (**1h**, **1h02min**) and at **1h05min** bear left (the right-hand path ascends to the Hotel Ca'n Costa below Lluc-Alcari). A few minutes more bring you to another well-shaded area with a round stone table and seats (but a sign above the table prohibits picnicking). Continue over the stone wall (you will see '57' painted in red on the rock), to find some stone steps down to a rocky platform and bathing area; you could end your walk here, if you like, and swim before returning to Cala de Deià.

To continue, follow the path past a stone-walled enclosure and climb some steps. At **1h20min** come to a high stone wall surrounding a house (below here there are two more excellent beaches — one of them popular with naturists). Turn up right here, to climb steps and then a path up to Lluc-Alcari, passing through two wooden gates near the bottom and an iron gate near the top. (There is also a path and steps from the other side of the house.) You reach the picturesque, bougainvillea-covered houses at the hamlet of Lluc-Alcari in **1h30min**. (*Short walk 1 turns back here.*) Turn up left, to meet the C710 at the KM59.6 marker (**1h45min**).

Turn right and follow the road to the KM60.2 marker, 10 minutes away (**1h55min**). The second half of the walk begins up the slope on the left, opposite the gates of Ca'n Puigserver. Walk up the main track for just under five minutes and then (soon after a bend to the right and opposite a house) turn left, up a rocky path marked by a cairn. You are now on the old wayfarers' route from Deià to Sóller, extensively used before the C710 was built. Keep ahead on the easily-followed path, and soon you will begin to get some excellent coastal views — do turn to admire them from time to time. At about **2h25min** come to a little cluster of houses known as Son Coll; the trail passes between them. Five minutes later, we can make a short detour to visit the Font de Son Coll, a mountain spring with a small stone seat: go left at the bottom of the wide stone steps, and descend some rather more ancient steps for a couple of minutes to find it.

Back on the main route, cross over a tarmac lane and continue ahead. Go through a gateway, after which the path descends gently through the woods, gradually veering away from the coast. If you come this way in spring, you will see violets, scarlet pimpernel, clematis, daisies,wild orchids, wild gladioli, and many other plants common only to the Balearics. Go through a couple more gates (at the second one there is a signpost back to Deià), and continue down onto a wider track, where you go right downhill. At about **3h25min**, after passing a huge sign 'Son Mico — Private Property', continue down towards the large mansion, but make a U-turn to the left just before it on a wide track that comes up from the C710. Then, almost immediately, turn right on a narrow grassy path through wasteland below the house and continue through an orange grove. At the end of the grove climb the wooden ladder placed for hikers; it takes you over a wall, and you rejoin the main route just by a pretty 13th-century chapel. Continue downhill, crossing a wide track. Beyond this track, the descent route is a fairly narrow, overgrown path. It soon widens out a bit, and later you will cross another wide track, after which the route acquires a rough concrete surface for about 100m/yds. Further downhill, just beyond stone engravings on the wall indicating 'Sóller' and 'Deià' (not easily spotted), descend some stony steps. (At the top of these steps, there is an old rusty sign nailed to a tree on the left, and a wide track heads off left just here — it leads to an excellent picnic spot on a pine-shaded grassy mound after some 20m/yds.

At **3h55min** you will have your first impressive views of the beautiful Sóller valley, surrounded by the island's highest peaks — including the Puig Major, the triangular summit of L'Ofre (Walks 9 and 12a), and the Serra d'Alfabia. A few minutes later, you cross above the 'wild-west' mountain railway, just above a tunnel. The path descends gradually into the valley, becoming a wide track further down. At the tall square house standing on its own on a corner, turn down left, and come out onto the main Sóller/Palma road almost opposite the petrol station (**4h25min**). If you are taking the bus back, go left down the main road, then take the first right after the petrol station. This brings you to the Plaça América (see Sóller plan on page 100) and the bus stop. Alternatively, walk into Sóller centre, and head right uphill to the train station (**4h30min**).

7 ES CASTELL D'ALARO

Distance/time: 7km/4.3mi; 2h30min (add 1h to visit the cave of Sant Antoni)

Grade: fairly easy, with some steepish slopes near the beginning. Outward climb of 300m/985ft. Danger of vertigo near the Cova de Sant Antoni, and do not enter the cave without the safety of a rope (there is an iron rope-hold at the entrance).

Equipment: hiking boots or strong shoes, water, picnic, sunhat; anorak in cold weather; torch and rope to visit the cave

How to get there and return: 🚗 to KM11.9 on the Alaró/Orient road; there is room to park several cars at various points nearby, or park in Orient village, and walk back to the starting point (1.5km).

Short walk: Orient — Es Pouet — Orient. 4.5km/2.8mi; 1h20min. You avoid the final ascent to the castle (100m/330ft), but still enjoy superb views.

Alternative walk: Alaró — Es Verger — Es Pouet — Castell d Alaró — Alaró. 9.5km/5.9mi; 4h; grade and equipment as main walk. Access/return: 🚌 to/from Alaró (departure times page 137). Walk up the main street in Alaró, turning right at the top on the Carrer Sollerich. Some 500m/yds after leaving the village, turn left up a tarmac lane signposted 'Es Pouet/Castillo'. Why not walk up in the afternoon, spend the night at the lodge, and the following morning explore around the Arab water tanks and the Cova de Sant Antoni, returning to Alaró in the afternoon? Good Mallorcan food can be had at the hikers' lodge (tel: 510480 for overnight stays), or at the Es Pouet restaurant half-way up, at the farm of Es Verger.

The once-magnificent Castell d'Alaró was so impregnable a fortress that an Arab commander-in-chief was able to hold out for almost two years after the Reconquest of Mallorca by Jaime I in 1229. Much of its old wall still stands, defiantly resisting ruin, blending reluctantly with the sheer reddish escarpments, thousands of feet above the plain. The mysterious cave of Sant Antoni on the precipice overhang jealously guards its many secrets, but allows the intrepid visitor a glimpse into the past ... who knows what rites were once performed in this strange place?

The Puig d'Alaró (left) and the Puig S'Alcadena frame the entrance to the Orient valley.

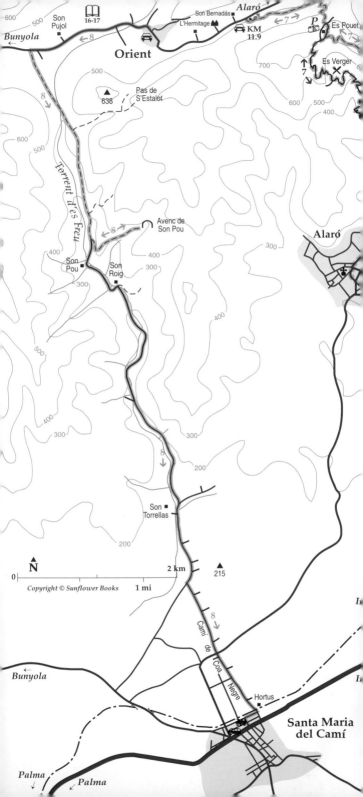

Start the walk at km11.9 on the Alaró/Orient road, opposite the farm of Son Bernadás. Go up through the access gate on the left (facing Orient), and veer left round a large water tank, to walk through terraces planted with olive trees. In **3min** see 'Castillo' painted on a rock at ground level, and keep ahead. After **10min** the path begins its steep zigzag climb through the woods. At **30min** you will come to an ideal picnic spot — a grassy outcrop to the right of the path (also an excellent vantage point from which to photograph the Orient valley). A little further up, go through an old gateway, giving access to a little clearing. This is also a good picnic spot if you prefer the shade, but there are no views. The path continues up to the right, and comes up to a wide track (**40min**). Turn up right here and, almost immediately, you will find yourself in a large clearing on the col known as Es Pouet (**45min**). You may be surprised to see cars parked here! It is possible to drive up from Alaró on the other side of the mountain, but not recommended for hire cars or nervous motorists! You may also come across Rita and Doris, two of the amiable transport donkeys from the hikers' lodge, patiently waiting for Josep to drive up in his jeep with provisions. They appreciate a pat on the nose.

Cross this clearing to the stone wall at the top, and find the beginning of the centuries-old stone-laid trail on your left (signposted). It has recently been repaired. Soon the awsome escarpments loom up ahead, as the trail becomes a series of stone steps winding ever higher towards the top. In **1h10min** go through the imposing archways and the castle entrance, to come onto a flatter, grassy, wooded area, from where the views are superb. On the left lies the incredibly beautiful and unspoilt valley of Sollerich, with its backcloth of high mountains, the peaks of L'Ofre (Walks 9 and 12a) and Massanella (Walk 14), and many others. To the right, the wide sweep of the plain reaches down as far as Palma and its huge circular bay. *Extra care* is needed near the unprotected precipitous drop on the left! It is wiser to admire the view to the north from a little further uphill, where there is a protecting wall. Then continue up to the hikers' lodge and the little pilgrims' chapel (**1h20min**).

Setting off for the castle ... seen from a distance below cherry trees ... we meet company ... and soon the castle looks closer.

For the intrepid, sure-footed walker, the route down to the Cova de Sant Antoni begins at the far end of the hikers' lodge: go through the metal gate by the side of some old latrines and follow the cairns, bearing right after five minutes. You descend the wooded slope towards the edge of the bluff. When you reach the old watchtower *(caution needed if you go inside),* turn left for about 20m/yds, to find a small hole in the rock. It doesn't seem to lead anywhere ... until you crouch down inside, and shine your torch to the right, to find the hidden entrance to the cave. If you have no rope, do *not* try to enter it: its dank floor, slippery with moss, slopes straight to the edge of the precipice! Content yourself with some good photos from the entrance. If you *are* carrying a rope and venture in, you will find a water tank fed by a small mountain spring near the top of the cave, as well as some beautiful stalactites. If you don't have a head for heights, and prefer safer walking, just visit the Arab water tanks *(algibes):* go through the metal gate by the latrines, and fork left in about three minutes. Another few minutes down and you're there. Take care at the steep drop beyond the lowest tank.

Return the same way (**2h 30min** — or 3h30min, if you visited the cave).

96

8 FROM ORIENT TO SANTA MARIA

See map pages 94-95   **Distance/time:** 14km/8.7mi; 4h30min

Grade: easy, gentle descent all the way (except for an ascent of some 160m/525ft about 35min into the walk). Thick undergrowth can obscure the path in places.

Equipment: hiking boots or stout walking shoes, long-sleeved shirt and long trousers, insect repellent, sunhat, suncream, water, picnic, whistle, compass; anorak in winter

How to get there: 🚗 private transport (taxi or friends) to Orient
To return: 🚌 (Timetable 10) or 🚐 (Timetable 6) from Santa Maria

Note: An impressive cavern lies en route, the Avenc de Son Pou. It is one of the largest on Mallorca, perhaps second only to the 'Campana', a cave near the Torrent de Pareis large enough to hold Palma's cathedral! Because of damage to stalactites, it is kept locked and may only be visited with a guide (telephone 270795 or 716450 well in advance, to arrange with Dr Matias Enseñat in Palma).

This lovely walk starts from the magical mountain village of Orient, set in a green and fertile valley untouched as yet by the masses, although frequently visited by hikers. Why not climb the stone steps up to the quiet little square by the churchyard before beginning your walk today? It's very picturesque.

Start out by heading west from Orient towards Bunyola. Walk along this quiet country lane for just over **20min**, then turn down a wide earthen track on the left (the second one you come to, just where the road begins to climb in bends). Go over the wooden step-ladder and continue along the walled-in track shown on page 63. Climb another ladder over a gate (**35min**), and cross the streambed further down — on stepping stones if water is flowing, although it is usually dry. (But first, if you wish to visit a delightful shaded picnic spot, do *not* cross the streambed — just continue ahead into the trees.) On the far side of the streambed, we begin to ascend the hillside, starting by the side of a large boulder; there are a few cairns here to guide you.

A few bends higher up (**55min**) the path forks; we opt for the path heading sharply to the right (paint waymarks), and now start to descend once more through abundant pampas grass and thick undergrowth. Occasional red or orange paint marks guide us (some of them crosses or numbers, eg X32). After another 20 minutes or so we reach the edge of the gorge, where the Torrent d'Es Freu flows through a wild and beautiful landscape. The path now continues above the course of the stream, and the further down you go, the more fantastic the scenery becomes — almost jungle-like with the occasional shriek of a bird echoing around the ravine and in the thickly-wooded

Olive press at Orient

slopes. Sometimes the path runs quite near the edge of the deep gorge; do *not* be tempted to peer down into the streambed, because the cliff-edges are soft and crumbly and could give way! At **1h35min** the path appears to peter out, but you can climb up left onto a wider path above the stone wall. Keep downhill for about another five minutes, watching for red paint daubs on the right-hand side of the path (by the side of a carob tree with spreading roots): these indicate the narrow trail up to the Avenc de Son Pou (**2h**). Visit this amazing cavern if you have made arrangements with Dr Enseñat in advance. Then return to the main path.

Our route down to Santa Maria from the carob tree is now quite straightforward; we descend past the houses of Son Pou and then follow the main track more or less in a straight run for some 3km, before forking left down the Camí de Coa Negre. Coming into Santa Maria just by the railway station, pass the Hortus Garden Centre, cross the railway lines, and turn right along the street to the station entrance. Alternatively, turn down left in front of the station to come to the main road and the bus stop by the Bar Comerç (**4h30min**).

The Orient valley

9 SOLLER • BINIARAIX • ES BARRANC • ES CORNADORS • L'OFRE • SOLLER

See map on reverse of touring map and plan of Sóller on page 100; see also photographs pages 27 and 109

Distance/time: 16km/9.9; 8h30min

Grade: very strenuous, but not technically difficult; ascent/descent of about 1150m/3775ft. The ascent of L'Ofre is steep and rocky.

Equipment: hiking boots, water, picnic, sunhat, anorak

How to get there and return: 🚌 (Timetable 11), 🚐 (Timetables 8, 9) to/from Sóller. Or 🚗 to/from Biniaraix and start at the 35min-point.

Short walk: from Biniaraix as far up the 'Barranc' as you wish and return. Easy; allow about 2h return. Equipment as above, but boots not necessary. 🚗 to/from Biniaraix, or walk from Sóller station.

Alternative walk: Cúber Lake — Sóller. 12km/7.4mi; 4h30min; easy ascent (130m/425ft); long descent (600m/1970ft). Sóller/Pollença 🚐 (Timetable 9; *note restricted service*) to KM34 on the C710. Follow the track from the Cúber Lake to L'Ofre farm, then turn right downhill for 'Sóller', to descend Es Barranc. Return: 🚌 or 🚐 as above.

During the preparation of this new edition, we had some sad news: the people at S'Arrom have decided to close the route through their farm to hikers. This was a blow to all of us, visitors and Mallorcans alike, as this walk was one of the classic circular hikes on the island. Sad, too, for Sóller, where the town council promotes hiking as an attractive winter holiday option. Consequently, I have had to modify this walk, and we must retrace our outgoing route. As some compensation, I include an ascent of the L'Ofre peak before descending the *barranc* back to Sóller. But while it is no longer a round trip, this is still one of the most beautiful walks on the island! Ideal for a clear, cool spring day, it can nevertheless can be enjoyed almost any time of year — there is plenty of shade in Es Barranc, and many clear pools to refresh your feet in summer. In addition to leafy glades and waterfalls, there are impressive cliffs, rocky mountains and spectacular views from the *mirador* on Es Cornadors (955m/3132ft) — certainly worth every bit of the effort it takes to climb up to it!

The walk begins in the Plaça de Sa Constitució (see town plan overleaf). Take the narrow Carrer de Sa Lluna and keep straight on for Biniaraix (signposted), crossing the bridge. Go left up the wide stone steps to the picturesque little square dominated by a large tree (**35min**). Stay in the same direction, along the Carrer Sant Josep (a sign on the wall says 'Lluc a pie') and, a minute later, turn right to find the start of our footpath (signposted 'Camí d'es Barranc'). Cross a small bridge at **45min**, the first of several, and continue gradually ascending this beautiful stone-laid trail, the

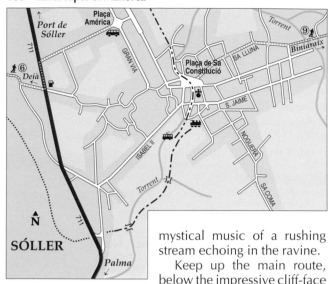

mystical music of a rushing stream echoing in the ravine.

Keep up the main route, below the impressive cliff-face above you on the right, and soon cross a second bridge over this curious stream, which occasionally disappears underground, so that one moment you can hear the water cascading over the rocks, and then all of a sudden you notice how silent it is... On the ascent, you will pass several old stone houses, once used by the olive pickers, and also many inviting rock pools. There are various water taps along the route, too; don't worry about the 'fizzy' appearance of the water, just let it settle before you drink it. Cross a third bridge at **1h45min** and, soon after, a fourth. You'll pass a large house with a very neat stone wall; turn around and see how high the olive terraces reach! At about **2h** the main path takes a sharp turn to the left; ignore the flat spur straight ahead, which soon ends. As you proceed, the views become more and more scintillating — Sóller village seems so far away now; you just have to keep stopping to look back down the ravine and across the Sóller basin ... as well as to catch your breath. Our stony trail passes below another fantastic cliff-face at about **2h30min** and, further along, as we round a bend, a rugged deep ravine appears below on the right, with the far-away sound of a rushing torrent coming up on the echo.

Not long after, we come to the iron gates that guard the Finca de L'Ofre. There are various signs: 'Private property', 'Beware bulls', etc, but you *are* allowed access here. Please make sure you close the gate behind you. The path now levels out and rounds the head of the canyon. At **3h** a sign

Es Barranc — a magical place to be, especially in the early morning, when the mists are rising and the sun's first rays slant an ethereal silvery glisten on the damp green fronds.

on the right, 'Mirador d'en Quesada', indicates our onward path — down to the right, across a little bridge. Beyond the bridge, the narrow earthen path soon starts to climb in earnest; this is an ascent in full sun on a good day; you will need your sunhat. Take a breather now and then, to turn and admire this beautiful high valley, with the L'Ofre farmhouse hiding below in the trees, the impressive triangular peak of the L'Ofre mountain (1090m/3575ft) rising in the northeast, and the wild and silent Serra d'Alfabia south of the valley.

Keep on up, passing two unusual rock formations in the form of columns, and in **3h30min** reach the pass between the two 'horns' of Es Cornadors, where the path divides. Turn right, up past the shelter, and scramble over the brow of the mountain, down to the precarious *mirador*. The views are truly breathtaking! The entire Sóller valley lies below you like a miniature toy world. Beyond lies the bay with its lighthouse, and all around you a magnificent panorama of the island's highest peaks — L'Ofre, the Puig Mayor, Massanella, the Serra d'Alfabia, the Teix...

Either picnic here, or back at the shelter, which offers some shade. Then return to where the path divides, this time going left, retracing your steps back down to the little bridge. From here follow signs to 'L'Ofre' — the triangular pine-wooded peak we have been admiring from the viewpoint. The route (marked with red paint) heads up through the trees, avoiding the farmhouses of L'Ofre, and soon comes up to a wide track just below the Coll de L'Ofre. *(The Alternative walk ascends this track.)* Carry on another couple of minutes up to the col (**4h35min**), for a sweeping view down to the lakes. Then use the notes for Walk 12a from the 1h30min-point (page 108) to climb the peak.

From the summit retrace your steps to the bridge and descend Es Barranc, to return to Sóller (**8h30min**).

10 MIRADOR DE SES BARQUES • SA COSTERA • CALA TUENT • SA CALOBRA

See map on reverse of touring map; see also photographs pages 28, 104-105

Distance/time: 16km/9.9mi; 6h30min

Grade: moderate, with several ascents and descents; the final stretch from Cala Tuent to Sa Calobra is strenuous and tedious. All good trails and tracks. Longest single ascent: 250m/820ft (Coll de Biniamar).

Equipment: hiking boots or stout walking shoes, water, picnic, sun-hat, insect repellent, swimwear and towel; anorak in cold weather

How to get there: 🚌 (Timetable 11), 🚆 (Timetable 8) or 🚗 to Sóller, then taxi or 🚐 (Timetable 9; *note restricted service*) to the Mirador de Ses Barques (or 🚐 direct from Pollença; Timetable 9 as above) *To return:* ⛴ from Sa Calobra (Timetable 13) to Port de Sóller. The boat calls at Cala Tuent some 10 minutes after leaving Sa Calobra *on Saturdays only;* it arrives at Port de Sóller in time to catch the bus to Pollença (Timetable 9) or tram to Sóller for the last train to Palma. *Note:* The boat runs all year round *in good weather* (see 'Weather', page 51), but will not take large groups. If you are more than four or five, opt for the Alternative walk described below.

Short walk: follow the main walk to the Font de Bálitx and return the same way. 4km/2.5mi; 1h10min; easy. Equipment: stout shoes, sun-hat, water, picnic. Access/return: 🚗 or Sóller/Pollença 🚐 to/from the Mirador de Ses Barques (Timetable 9; *note restricted service*).

Alternative walk: follow the main walk to Sa Costera and return the same way. 12km/7.4mi; under 5h. Equipment and grade as main walk; access/return as *Short walk.*

The Mirador de Ses Barques is a very scenic spot on the mountain road above Sóller. From a height of over 400m/1310ft, we can take in a magnificent panorama of the village and port below, reflected in the shimmering blue Mediterranean and surrounded by the highest mountains of the sierra. The *mirador* is also well known for its orange juice, freshly-squeezed from the delicious orange

Near Bálitx de Dalt

Waterfall and coastal landscape at Sa Costera

groves of the Sóller valley. Why not enjoy a sparkling glass of 'sunshine' before embarking on this hike?

The walk begins here at the viewpoint, up the steps to the right of the gates (signposted). Keep left twice, and then go through a metal gate (**10min**). Five minutes later you join a wide track and head right. Approach the old farmstead of Bálitx de Dalt (Upper Bálitx), but turn down right through the gateway just below the big house. Now you are in the incredibly beautiful valley of Bálitx, where footpaths wind away over the hills, and a myriad of silvery-leaved olive trees populate a thousand terraces.

At **30min**, just on a bend to the left, take a stone-laid trail straight down to the Font de Bálitx, a hidden mountain spring; this short cut also avoids a couple of bends in the track. To rejoin the track, turn down left from the spring (the path is a little narrow at the bottom). Continue to the right along the main route, passing the huge abandoned farm of Bálitx d'en Mig (Middle Bálitx; **45 min**).

In **1h15min** come to the farm of Bálitx d'Avall (Lower Bálitx), where María and Guillermo will welcome you to another fresh orange juice, inside the cool interior of this big old farmhouse. They also sell lovely home-made marmalade, little bags of sun-dried apricots, almonds, *hierbas* (a Mallorcan alcoholic drink made with fres' herbs), and many other tempting things. An overnight st' here, with a Mallorcan cooked supper, bed and break' and the use of a stone swimming pool with a breatht; view will not break the bank, should you wish to tu into a two-day adventure, but it is best to telephone hand to check they have a room (tel: 634240 o 908 631011; the summer months are their 'low

From the farm, turn down right and descen

103

trail, to cross the streambed. Then begin the arduous ascent of about 30 minutes up to the Coll de Biniamar. At just under **2h** you will reach the pass, where the way levels out a bit and is also refreshed by a cool sea breeze. Now descend again and, about five minutes later (by a bend to the right), find your path down to Sa Costera, where there is an abandoned house. The path begins through a gateway to the left of the track; it takes about half an hour to get down to the house. Just looking at the beautiful view down over the bay of Es Racó de Sa Taleca and the shimmering blue waters erases all thoughts of the climb back up from your mind… Find the mountain spring hiding in a dark tunnel just up on a ridge behind the house, and enjoy a picnic lunch under the young olive tree.

From Sa Costera, climb back up to the main track (**3h**), then turn down left to follow the coastal route. About halfway to Cala Tuent, watch for a small blue arrow on a rock, indicating a path down to the sea. At the bottom of this path, near the abandoned hydroelectric plant, there's an incredible mountain spring … gushing out tons of precious water into the sea. Return to the main coastal path and continue over the hill at the end of the bay, later keeping right where the stone-laid trail divides.

You come down into Cala Tuent at **4h30min**; this is a truly boring place — the only spot of life being the restaurant just above the beach. Just past the restaurant, take the second set of steps down onto the beach, to avoid a long walk round. Cross to the road on the far side, and brace yourself for the long, arduous walk up the tarmac (or wait for the boat if it's Saturday). At the top of the climb you come to the 13th-century chapel of Sant Llorenç. (There is a shortcut back down to the road here, at the right of the gate, but at time of writing it had been closed off.)

You should reach Sa Calobra at about **h30min**. Relaxing now, on the boat ck to Port de Sóller, contemplate the d and rugged mountainous scenery ted in the deep blue waters — a truly cular landscape of Mallorca.

nd 11 end here at the mouth of the Pareis — the setting for Picnic 11.

11 ES TORRENT DE PAREIS

See map on reverse of touring map; see also photos pages 29, 56
Distance/time: 7km/4.3mi; 4h
Grade: difficult and tough; *only for expert mountain walkers with some climbing experience.* **You must be able to swim.**
Equipment: hiking boots, change of clothing in waterproof bag, towel, water, picnic, sunhat, suncream, torch, whistle, anorak, short rope
How to get there: 🚌 (Timetable 11), 🚐 (Timetables 8, 9) or 🚗 to Sóller or Port de Sóller, then Sóller/Pollença 🚐 (Timetable 9; *note restricted service*) to the Escorca restaurant at KM25 on the C710 (or 🚐 direct to the restaurant, if coming from Pollença)
To return: ⛴ from Sa Calobra (Timetable 13) to Port de Sóller for connection with ongoing transport (as above).
Short walk: Es Torrent de Pareis from Sa Calobra. Explore the gorge from its mouth. This is easy but, once at the first high boulders, do *not* attempt to continue without adequate equipment. Take sunhat, swimwear, suncream, wading shoes, water and picnic. Access/return: ⛴ (Timetable 13) or 🚗 to/from Sa Calobra.

Following the course of the Torrent de Pareis gorge is perhaps the island's most spectacular excursion on foot ... except for the daring adventure of its twin gorge, Sa Fosca, where only speleologists dare to penetrate the narrow cascading underground watercourse. Our hike down the Torrent de Pareis, however, is *not* for the inexperienced; you will have to scramble over slippery rocks, wade through icy pools, and maybe even swim — if you venture down here after a rainy period (flash floods are not unknown). But this is a walk for the summer months only, May to September.

Start the walk opposite the Escorca restaurant. Go through the small green metal gate at the west side of the layby for the St Pere chapel, near the KM25.2 marker. (There is a notice here in several languages warning of the difficulty of this hike.) At **10min** climb over a small iron gate and follow the wall on your left. Do *not* curve right on the clear, slightly-raised path encountered in a couple of minutes, but keep straight downhill until the path turns sharp left, to begin its descent into the gorge (**15min**). At some rocks further down, turn left again, and then right, following the red paint marks. The path now winds down into the gorge, which is already visible.

You'll reach the *voltes llargues* (the long bends) in **30min**. At **1h** the path passes below the branches of a fig tree: some 20m/yds or so further along, paint waymarks lead you off the path, down through rocks and tall pampas grass. Less than 10 minutes more should find you at the bottom, in the bed of the Torrent de Lluc. Now turn left to follow the streambed, amongst strewn rocks and boulders. Watch for a grassy path on the left that will lead you above some impassable rocks and then down again — into the wider Entreforc (**1h20min**), where the Torrent de Lluc unites with the waters coming from Sa Fosca, to form the Torrent de Pareis (the 'twin torrents').

Down here, dwarfed by sheer rock faces and vertical cliffs, the hiker is surrounded by a fantastic wild landscape; the blue of the sky above seems far, far away ... and the screech of wild birds and the occasional bleat of a mountain goat echo loudly around the canyon. A large rock here in the middle of S'Entreforc bears a red-painted cross indicating four directions: to the southeast is Lluc; to the northwest Sa Calobra, our destination; to the south lies Sa Fosca (the 'dark place') ... and to the north, where there is a sheer rock wall, we are advised: *'Millor no anarí'* ('better not go')!

To begin down the gorge, continue to the right, to find the small path leading uphill through long grass (one or two red arrows). From here, explanations are superfluous. It's simply a matter of finding the best way down the course of the streambed, over rocks and boulders and through narrow passes, skirting the rock pools if you can.

Once at Sa Calobra bay (**4h**), go left up some stone steps just before reaching the pebble beach, and walk through two tunnels in the rock. This will bring you to another beach and the landing jetty for your boat back to Port de Sóller .

12 TWO WALKS FROM CÚBER LAKE

See map on reverse of touring map; see also photos pages 63, 93

Walk a (Cúber Lake— Coll de L'Ofre — L'Ofre — Cúber Lake):
12km/7.4mi; 5h. Quite easy ascent of 100m/330ft up to the Coll de L'Ofre, but the last 30min stretch (another 200m/650ft) up steep rocky terrain to L'Ofre peak is strenuous. Equipment: hiking boots, water, picnic, suncream, sunhat; anorak in winter. Access/return: Sóller/ Pollença 🚌 (Timetable 9; *note restricted service*) or 🚗 to Cúber Lake (KM34 on the C710); park by the lake. See walking notes page 108.

Short walk a (Circuit of Cúber Lake): 4km/2.5mi; 1h; easy. Equipment: stout shoes, binoculars, water. Access/return as Walk a. Follow the main walk to the 40min-point. Once over the stile, turn back left along the track to circle the lake. Good area for bird watching.

Alternative walk a (Cúber Lake— Coll de L'Ofre — Orient valley overlook — Cúber Lake): 12.5km/7.8mi; 5h. Quite easy ascent of 100m/330ft up to the Coll de L'Ofre; this version cuts out the rough ascent to L'Ofre peak. Access/return and equipment as Walk a, but stout walking shoes will suffice. Follow the main walk to the base of L'Ofre mountain (1h50min), then continue along the track for some 15min more, winding down the south side of L'Ofre. You come to a stone house and grassy platform with wonderful vistas across the Orient valley to the two bluffs shown on page 93 and the plain beyond them. Return the same way.

Walk b (Cúber Lake — Tossals Verds — Lloseta): 16km/10mi; 5h; easy descent of 650m/2130ft on good trails and wide tracks. Equipment: hiking boots or stout shoes, water, picnic (but see *Note* below), suncream, sunhat; anorak in winter. Access as Walk a; return by 🚌 (Timetable 10). If travelling by 🚗, leave the car at Lloseta and take a taxi up to Cúber to start the walk (arrange this beforehand, as there is no taxi rank in Lloseta). See walking notes page 109.

Note: Tossals Verds is a government-run hikers' refuge in a beautiful setting, where walkers can stay the night. It is also possible to order cooked meals (in advance) if you want to make a day of it. Tel: 182027.

Alternative walk b (Cúber Lake— Font d'es Prat — Font de Sa Basola — Cúber Lake): 11km/6.8mi; 4h; easy. Equipment as Walk b. Access/ return as *Walk a*. Follow Walk b as far as the Font de Sa Basola (1h45min) and return the same way.

The L'Ofre peak (1090m/3575ft) — goal of Walk a — is a triangular, pine-wooded mountain with a bare rocky top, boasting some of the most marvellous views up in the Serra de Tramuntana, and it is reached without much effort from our starting point at Cúber Lake. It is also an excellent setting for sighting some of the bigger birds of prey — black vultures, red kites, and eagles ... soaring over the still waters or circling high on the thermals between these craggy highest peaks of the sierra. On the other hand, Walk b is one of my favourites. It's relatively easy, yet takes you through some enchanting scenery, as you descend from the heights down towards the plain, through ever-changing landscapes — rocky mountain trails, woodlands and streams, craggy gorges and sweeping valleys.

Start Walk a from the small parking area at KM34 on the C710 and go through the access gate onto the wide track. Almost immediately, veer off right, to follow the path around the top end of the lake. It becomes an earthen track. A few minutes further along, just where logic tells you to keep right, go *left,* to find an elevated, rough track that borders the north side of the lake. Serenity and beauty are just two of the many words one could use to describe the sensation of walking along here beside the water, where occasionally a trout will leap up out of the deep blue and splash down again, and the far side of the lake reflects the rugged ridge and the peaks of La Rateta (1107m/3631ft) and Na Franquesa (1060m/3477ft).

At **30min** we pass the far end of the lake; there is a stone refuge with a picnic table just across the water. Continuing, we soon cross a small stream, after which the way veers uphill to the right and we climb a stile (**40min**) and come onto the wide track that leads to L'Ofre. *(Short walk a turns left here.)* Turning right, we follow the track for a few minutes to come to the gates of the L'Ofre farmlands. The L'Ofre farm breeds cattle, and from here onwards you will be walking across open countryside where both bulls and cows roam freely, unperturbed by the presence of hikers. However, there is a sign at the gate to warn you and requesting that you do not go off the main route. Go down the steps to the small access gate, and continue along the track, which undulates between the high ridges of Na Franquesa to the left and the Torrellas to the right. At **1h10min**, after a bend to the left, we leave the main track, following red paint spots marking a narrow earthen path up through pretty woodlands. A gradual climb takes us up to the Coll de L'Ofre (**1h30min**). Turn around here for a spectacular panorama back down over our route through the valley, to Cúber Lake glistening in the distance, with the imposing slopes of the Puig Major in the background.

Continuing along to the right, just past the col, one can veer off the track for a few minutes and head downhill to the right, for another impressive panoramic view — this time over the Sóller basin. There is even a telescope here. Back on the track, walk downhill for a couple of minutes and then take the track off left, which rounds the base of L'Ofre. We eventually come to an 'opening', where the track veers round to the left and through a col (**1h50min**); off to the right, a narrow path takes us to the edge of the

View from L'Ofre peak, towards the lakes and the Puig Major

rocks on the south side of L'Ofre. Here another telescope affords a sweeping view over the beautiful Orient valley. On the left of the track, blue and red paint marks indicate a path up through the trees — the beginning of the tough ascent to the top. *(The Alternative walk continues straight on down the track at this point.)*

To climb L'Ofre, we follow the paint marks, soon coming out of the woods, to start a steepish (but not too difficult) ascent up the rocky slope. We arrive on the bare smooth rocks of the summit at **2h20min**. Wonder of wonders — the panorama will astound you! Both lakes are clearly visible far below to the northeast, with the high crags of the Puig Major as a backcloth. Sóller bay and its valley lie at our feet, and many peaks of the Serra de Tramuntana stretch away onto the east and west horizons. The vast plain spreads out to the south, dotted with distant towns and villages. A great reward for not *such* a big effort!

To return, descend to the wide track and retrace your steps to the gates of L'Ofre farm. Then continue straight ahead, rounding the opposite side of the lake and crossing the dam, back to the C710 and your transport (**5h**).

Start Walk b by descending the road, walking from the Cúber Lake towards the Gorg Blau. Where the water channel (*'tubería'* on the map) goes under the road, pick up the maintenance path alongside it, heading in a northeasterly direction. Now we follow the water channel, with the C710 winding away below us, and admire the magnificent views down over the Gorg Blau lake as we contour round the mountain slopes. After **30min** or so we come to a bridge signposted 'Tossals Verds'. Cross the bridge, and continue up through the woods on the old cobbled steps (the ancient wayfarers' route from Sóller to Lluc), passing various *sitjas*, remains of the old charcoal industry (see page 60). Soon we reach the Coll d'es Coloms (Pigeons' Pass). Just over the col, ignore a little path off right into the woods (it leads up to the summit of the Tossals mountain). Continuing gently downhill through a dappled landscape of holm oak woods, at **55min** we turn off right at another signpost to Tossals Verds, still descending. If you wish to visit the Font d'es Prat (see Walk 13, page 112), keep on the main route for about another 10 minutes, then return to this point.

Our route now takes us through a very pretty landscape of woodlands and streams, and we soon cross a wooden bridge over the tinkling waters. A couple of minutes further down, we cross the stream again, this time on large stepping- stones, to continue along a beautiful old rocky mountain trail as it rounds the eastern face of the large craggy Tossals mountain. Where the trail makes a sharp bend down to the left, lift your eyes for a minute to look across to the rocky crags opposite, and you will see the old aqueduct which was built to carry the famous Canaleta de Massanella (notes pages 60-61 and 113) on its way down to the plain — this is the best view of it. Carrying on, taking time to admire the panoramic views of the plain that have opened up before us, our route eventually becomes less rocky and goes through an opening in an old stone wall. We emerge on the slopes of Sa Basola where, just uphill from the path, the old well of Sa Basola sits on an open incline (**1h45min**). This is a very pretty place in spring, when the field is a mass of high pink asphodels blowing in the breeze. *(The Alternative walk turns back here.)*

Refreshed after a drink, we continue along the grassy path over the brow of the hill, passing by the ruins of an old farmstead (Les Cases Velles) down to the right. Panoramic views surround us as we march on; far-reaching vistas ahead show us the distant green fields of the Orient valley and, to the right, high rocky ridges — from Tossals mountain to the L'Ofre peak (Walk a). Below us lies a once-farmed, secluded valley, where there are still a few almond trees on the terraced slopes, and drystone walls reach high up the hillside. At **1h55min** ignore a fork up left off the main path, signposted 'Es Pinetons'; it is a rough and little-used route over the hill and down onto the plain.

Continuing along the stony path, you find yourself in a 'rock garden' — all manner of flowering shrubs border the way — bright yellow gorse bushes, wild thyme, wild sage, *Euphorbias* and *Hypericum* throw splashes of colour over the limestone rocks, as we descend ever more gently towards the next valley. Further down, the path goes through a 'gateway' of sorts, and soon begins a more serious descent, twisting and turning through a series of rocky bends, down to the hikers' refuge of Tossals Verds (**2h20min**). Here, you can enjoy your picnic on the grassy terrace where there are a few wooden tables and benches, overlooking the most marvellous view, or eat inside if the weather isn't good. You can buy hot drinks too. Alternatively, enjoy a cooked meal if you ordered it beforehand.

To continue on towards the plain, we leave the refuge by the large gates and walk down the wide track — a wonderful winding route through a myriad of olive trees on sloping terraces, still surrounded by a mountainous landscape. Further down, the track snakes between the high sides of a very impressive gorge, crosses a boulder-strewn stream via a bridge, and comes down into foothills.

At **3h30min** we climb a stile over a fence at a small parking area, then continue along a tarmac lane. Cross a small bridge and continue through fields and woodlands. It is now fairly level walking, with the streambed on our left; soon we can see the impressive rocky pine-covered cliffs of S'Alcadena to the right — one of the twin bluffs visible from L'Ofre peak or from the plain (see photograph page 93). At **4h45min** the narrow lane meets the PM211 (the Lloseta/Alaró road) on a wide bend. Here we keep straight ahead, ignoring the first left turn. Eventually we turn left into Lloseta on the main road, just before the railway bridge. The station is just a little further along (**5h**).

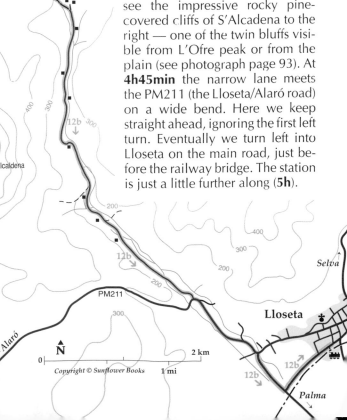

13 CUBER LAKE • FONT D'ES PRAT • COLL D'ES PRAT • LLUC

See map on reverse of touring map; see also photograph page 61

Distance/time: 14km/8.7mi; 4h35min

Grade: strenuous, but not difficult, with an ascent of some 500m/ 1640ft up to the Coll d'es Prat. Good tracks and paths all the way. The descent to Lluc is easy, but very stony.

Equipment: hiking boots or stout walking shoes, sunhat, water bottle, picnic; anorak in cold weather

How to get there: Sóller/Pollença 🚍 (Timetable 9; *note restricted service*) or 🚗 to the Cúber Lake at KM34 on the C710

To return: 🚍 (Timetable 3) from Lluc to Palma (or to Inca, to connect with the 🚂 to Palma; Timetable 10), or 🚍 back along the C710 (Timetable 9; *note restricted service*) to your car at Cúber Lake

Short walk: Cúber Lake — Font d'es Prat — Cúber Lake. 6.5km/4mi; 2h; easy; stout shoes will suffice. Access/return: 🚗 or Sóller/Pollença 🚍 (Timetable 9; *note restricted service*) to/from Cúber Lake. Follow the main walk to the 1h-point, then return the same way.

Note: A fee is payable at Comafreda (see *Note* for Walk 14, page 115), but the guard may have left if you pass through in the afternoon.

The tinkling of sheep bells, the wind whispering through the trees, and the gentle music of flowing waters are the only sounds that penetrate the impressive silence of the central mountains of the sierra. The magnificent landscapes change continually, as we admire the Gorg Blau lake (the 'Blue Gorge') from our elevated path alongside the water-course, walk through the holm oak woods over the 'Pigeons' Pass', and then ascend towards the north face of the Massanella mountain, habitat of great black vultures. This climb takes us through a wilderness of strewn rocks and tall pampas grass towards the highest mountain pass on the island, the Coll d'es Prat (1205m/3952ft): from here, stretching away to the horizon on both sides in a series of high craggy peaks, practically all of the sierra is visible.

Start out by following Walk 12b (page 109) to the **55min**-point, where that walk turns off right for Tossals Verds. Keep left here, down the main route, which becomes much more stony, and go through a gap in the stone wall of the abandoned farm of Es Prat de Massanella. Keep straight ahead until you come to a junction of paths:

Passing above the farm of Almallutx on the watercourse, above the Gorge Blau

Font d'es Prat de Massanella: the date 1748, engraved down inside the well, is the year in which work on the Canaleta de Massanella began.

to the right, an overgrown path leads to the famous Canaleta de Massanella*, to the left lies the Font d'es Prat, and our route to the col and Massanella lies straight ahead. But first let's go left to see the mountain spring of Es Prat, set in a large shady clearing. The crystal-clear waters from inside the well are refreshing to drink, and you can refill your water bottle here for the rest of the journey.

The next stage of the hike begins back at the junction: go over the 'bridge' to find the beginning of the narrow earthen path that leads up to the Coll d'es Prat (some cairns mark the start). It ascends gently at first, and then becomes steeper, crossing a *sitja* at **1h35min** and passing two more springs, one with a drinking trough for animals. Stay on the higher of the two paths, which soon emerges from the woods to continue up the long bare slope amongst rocks and high grass. This red earth path can become a raging torrent in heavy rain! You can now see the saddle up ahead, and at about **2h** the path comes up onto the cobbled mountain highway, another part of the original Sóller-Lluc trail. From time to time, stop to look back at the magnificent mountain panorama behind you; many peaks are visible, including the Tossals group, La Rateta, the triangular peak of L'Ofre (Walks 9 and 12a), and the Teix (Walk 5).

*If you have time, you may like to see this old watercourse (its history is outlined on page 60). The way is overgrown, but keep ahead, with the streambed on your left. After about 300m/yds, you will come to some pools of water and the beginning of the *canaleta*, now sadly encased in piping. There was a great outcry from conservationists when this national monument was 'modernised' in 1983. It used to be a wonderful adventure to follow the *canaleta* from here when it was free-flowing: one climbed the high stone wall of Es Molinot (the 'big old mill') and had to proceed very carefully along a narrow stretch for about five minutes, as the channel rounded the side of the mountain (see photograph page 61). *If you're not subject to vertigo, and you're sure-footed,* a few minutes along from the wall will bring you far enough to be able to see the arched aqueduct that carries the *canaleta* across a ravine — still a beautiful sight, though overgrown. Although the channel continues round mountains and through tunnels down to Mancor del Valle, about 6km southeast, I would advise you to go no further than the aqueduct.

Looking east from the Coll d'es Prat

At **2h40min** the route levels out by another stone wall which divides this valley in two. This is the Coll d'es Prat. The impressive rocky northern face of Massanella looms up on the right, and you may well see silhouetted hikers up on the peak (Walk 14), the highest accessible point for walkers on the island. And a scan of the skies may well reveal the silent glide of a black vulture or two circling high above you. Go through the gap in the wall, and … another fabulous panorama unfolds before you! The huge round massif of the Puig Tomir (Walk 16), surrounded by many other mountain peaks, stretches out below you as far as the rugged northeastern coastline, with the craggy tops of the Cavall Bernat on a distant horizon to your left, and the wide sweep of Alcúdia's bay to your right.

A few minutes further down the far side of the pass will bring you to the first of the snowhouses (*cases de neu;* see page 58). This one is in fairly good condition and affords a picnic place sheltered from the strong winds that sometimes blow through the 'funnel' of the high pass. There is also a freshwater spring just below.

The route down to Lluc follows this long, winding rocky trail as it zigzags down into the beautiful Comafreda valley, where no sound but the tinkle of sheep bells breaks the silence. The path becomes a track at just under **4h** and later passes below the Comafreda farmhouse. Go over the ladder at the gate, and wind down left to come onto the Lluc/Inca road at **4h35min**. Go left and over the bridge, to come to the petrol station and refreshments at the roadside café while you wait for the bus to Inca, or walk on to the C710 for the Sóller/Pollença bus.

14 PUIG DE MASSANELLA — CLASSIC ASCENT

See map on reverse of touring map

Distance/time: 10km/6.2mi; 5h

Grade: strenuous, only for experienced mountain walkers. A tough climb of 780m/2560ft over rocky paths (at times not easily seen). Risk of thick mists falling; possibility of vertigo at the summit

Equipment: hiking boots, long trousers, suncream, sunhat, water, picnic, water-purifying tablets, compass, whistle, torch; cardigans and anorak in winter; shorts and T-shirt in summer

How to get there and return: 🚌 to/from Lluc (Timetable 3) or 🚐 to/from Inca (Timetable 10), where you can connect with the same bus. Do not go all the way to Lluc, but ask to be put off at the Lluc petrol station, at the Coll de Sa Bataia. Alternatively, Sóller/Pollença 🚌 (Timetable 9; *note restricted service*): ask for the Lluc petrol station. Or 🚗 to/from the Coll de Sa Bataia on the PM213 (where there is a petrol station); park opposite the roadside café.

Note: A small fee is being charged to hikers going through the farm of Comafreda on their way to Massanella, due to large amounts of litter being left by local weekend trippers. At time of writing this is 500 ptas per person (1000 ptas for mountain bikes).

The Puig de Massanella is that double-peaked, high rocky mountain in the centre of the Serra de Tramuntana. The second highest mountain in Mallorca, its peaks reach up to 1348m and 1352m (4430ft). An incredible panorama is seen from the summit — almost all of the island — and, on a clear day, the islands of Menorca and Cabrera are also visible — worth every bit of the effort it takes to reach the top!

The walk begins at Lluc petrol station at the Coll de Sa Bataia, south of Lluc. Walk down the PM213 towards Inca, crossing the narrow bridge. You come to wide iron gates on the right, just past the bend. A stone engraved with 'Puig de Massanella' lies to the left of the gates, but is often

Comafreda farm

obscured by undergrowth. Go through the access gate, and keep along the wide track as it winds up and veers right (ignore the track straight ahead on the first sharp bend). At **15min**, where two tracks go straight ahead, turn sharp right uphill on an older track, towards the Comafreda farm. After 10 minutes you'll reach a gate; this is where a guard will charge you the fee for passing through the farmlands of Comafreda.

Just before the track goes through a stone wall (the descent route of Walk 13), turn up sharp left, along a shady earthen track. Now follow the red paint marks; the way becomes more rocky, going through the remains of an old stone wall and crossing a *sitja*. Make sure you follow the red paint marks; they eventually bring you up onto the main track again at about **40min**. Turn up left and follow this wide track through the woods, coming up to the Pas de N'Arbona (832m/2730ft) at **55min**. Here the high rocky crags of the Puig de N'Alí (1038m/3405ft) rise above you on the left. There are two large engraved stones with arrows here at the pass: one arrow points straight on towards Mancor, another back to Lluc, and a third up right towards the 'Puig'(de Massanella) — today's route. Turn right then, and follow the red paint spots as they lead you up through the trees, now more steeply. At **1h05min** you'll see a red 'II' painted on a boulder on a bend. Further up, the view begins to attract our attention as the trees thin out, and it is necessary to stop for a breather from time to time to admire the splendid scenery — the plain stretching out down to the southern coastline, the city of Palma with its wide bay, and a hazy horizon hiding the sea.

Continue up through sparse trees and clumps of pampas grass; our path has become very rocky indeed! Keep looking for the red spots to guide you. At **1h30min** come to the mountain crossroads of S'Avenc del Camí, where there is a small deep pit on the right of the path. (Someone has thoughtfully covered it with a huge rock to avoid accidents.) A few steps further up, another engraved stone indicates two possible ascent routes: straight on to the 'Font de S'Avenc' or up right to the summit. Since a circular route is always more interesting, let's do the tour in a clockwise direction, first visiting the spring — a good place to picnic and recuperate energy for the final assault. (It is also easier to follow the route this way round.)

Our path to the spring climbs the stony slopes, bearing left at first, and then crosses a treeless expanse of white jagged limestone rocks, bearing slightly right. Watch carefully for the cairns and red paint spots — essential here for keeping to the route. Soon after climbing over higher rocks, you'll come to the Font de S'Avenc (**2h**), a marvellous place, just like an Aladdin's Cave! Hidden deep in the mountainside at 1200m/3940ft, this spring bubbles fresh, cool filtered water all year round. It is best visited in spring and early summer, near midday, when the sun is overhead and its rays illuminate the dark, dank steps that lead down into the mountain (but further down you will need your torch).

An engraved indication stone near the entrance to the spring points the way to the summit, which is only attained after a good deal of clambering over high rocks. One feels so minute on this mountain, nothing more than a speck of humanity, crawling up over the massive moonscaped rock-face like an ant labouring over a boulder. However, at **2h50min** you'll reach the summit! And the panorama is, of course, worth every minute of effort spent — the whole island lies below you, a magical landscape of mountains, hills and valleys. You are now on the highest accessible point on Mallorca, since the summit of the Puig Major is out of bounds due to the radar station. In your wonder and admiration, *don't forget to be careful* — just below the summit is one of the island's deepest snowpits.

To descend, face the plain: you should be able to see a small tableland below, to the left of the peak. Bear left and make your way down over rocks and boulders towards it, (if mists are obscuring the view, bear east). Some 20 minutes downhill, it's easy to find the flat earthen path. This winds southeast and then begins a rocky zigzag descent, coming back down to the Avenc del Camí. Now follow your outgoing route down to the left, passing Comafreda, and coming back down onto the Lluc/Inca road at **5h**.

Clocktower at Lluc Monastery

15 LLUC • BINIFALDO • AUCANELLA • BINIBONA • CAIMARI

Map begins on the reverse of the touring map; ends page 120; see also photographs pages 117, 122

Distance/time: 14km/8.7mi; 6h

Grade: fairly easy, but quite long; ascent of 150m/490ft and descent of 400m/1310ft. Extra care required on the loose, jagged rocks above the streambed.

Equipment: hiking boots or strong shoes, water, picnic, sunhat, suncream, insect repellent, long trousers, long-sleeved shirt; anorak in cold weather

How to get there: 🚌 to Lluc (Timetable 3) or 🚂 to Inca (Timetable 10), where you can connect with the same bus. Alternatively, Sóller/Pollença 🚌 (Timetable 9; *note restricted service*) to the KM16.4 marker on the C710, by the SEFOBASA picnic area, from where you follow notes for *Walk 17* on pages 123-124 to the 35min-point. Then then turn right, walk to the Binifaldó house, and pick up the walk below at the 1h-point. If travelling by 🚗, park at the bottom end of Caimari in time to take the Inca/Lluc bus (Timetable 3) up to Lluc.

To return: 🚌 (Timetable 3) from Caimari — to Inca for the Palma train or for buses to Palma, Pollença or Alcúdia, or to Lluc for the Sóller/Pollença bus. Or pick up your waiting car at Caimari.

Short walk: Caimari — Binibona — Caimari. 5km/3mi; 1h15min; easy; stout shoes will suffice. Access/return: 🚌 to/from Caimari (Timetable 3), or 🚗. From Caimari, follow signposting to Binibona along a country lane with far-reaching views, and return the same way.

Thankfully, there are still some quiet spots in this crazy, stressed-out world of ours, as we shall discover on this walk. From Binifaldó we descend alongside a rocky streambed, to come onto the beautiful, silent, south side of the Tomir mountain, where some old stone houses while away the time on a grassy plateau high above the plain — a very romantic picnic spot! Later we wind down through thick undergrowth, zigzag down a rocky trail and walk through the lower woodlands to the picturesque little hamlet of Binibona, before following a country lane to Caimari.

Start the walk at Lluc, taking the road back out of the monastery. After some 100m/yds, turn left into a wide entrance. Then turn right immediately, along a path past a stone house, and go through the gate of the football pitch and *fronton* court. At the far end you come out onto a wide track. Now follow this track, passing below a camp site and picnic area, then winding gently uphill to the C710 (**25min**). Turn left along the road for about 100m/yds, then cross over and follow the rough tarmac lane signposted to Binifaldó and Menut (at the KM17.4 marker stone). After a few minutes you will come to two sets of gates by the forestry station of Menut; opt for the left-hand one, using the access gate if this is closed (as it will be at weekends).

118

On the southern slopes of the Puig Tomir, by the old farm of Aucanella. The area is a mass of daisies in spring.

Follow this lovely woodland lane for a while, passing the big old stone house of Binifaldó (**1h**) and continuing uphill in bends to the gates of the Binifaldó water-bottling plant (**1h15min**). *(The ascent of the Tomir mountain, Walk 16, begins here, to the right of the gate.)*

Go through the lower wooden gateway, down a wide woodland trail that descends gently in a series of S-bends. At **1h30min** the track takes a sharp bend to the right over a kind of 'bridge'. Here we leave the main route: we also go right, but *below* the track, crossing the rocks of the streambed to find the beginning of a narrow path. (If you are agile and don't mind boulder-hopping, you can go directly down the streambed from the 'bridge' and pick up the notes again at the 2h15min-point.) Our path ascends through trees at first, and eventually becomes very rocky. Look carefully for the cairns, camouflaged amongst the loose sharp rocks and not easily seen. This path runs some 50m/150ft above the right-hand bank of the stream, then dips down over very loose rocks, back down to the tree-line, and crosses the streambed again at **2h15min**.

Now we follow a narrower, flatter path from the streambed through high *Cistus*, being sure to watch for the red paint marks. If you come this way in spring, the strong and fragrant scent of the rock roses and other mountain flora is almost overpowering, while the lazy drone of insects and the song of the nightingale seem only to accentuate the unbelievable peace on this wilder, south side of Tomir. Guided by the red spots, keep ahead through a gap in an old stone wall into an area that used to belong to the Aucanella farm. Follow the route carefully as it winds through the trees, turning left at a cairn and red paint spot, down past an ancient drinking trough. You approach the back of the large abandoned house of Aucanella at about **2h30min**. The structure is still quite solid, although some of the beams are rotted and ceilings have caved in, so it would be safer to picnic in front of the house on the grassy terraces, where there is also some shade under the trees.

To continue, make your way down the terraces in front

119

of the house, and go through the gap in the stone wall directly below. Now turn right, and follow the narrow, worn footpath across the fields in a southwesterly direction, coming to the end of the last open field at the head of a valley, where a rocky path begins by the side of a tree. Here's where you should put on your long trousers, and spread generous amounts of insect repellent over any areas of bare skin to avoid picking up ticks (in hot weather), as you'll find this descending path quite overgrown with tall pampas grass and thick undergrowth.

Further down, the surroundings change, as we go over a rocky pass, and zigzag down a long stony trail, finally coming down into the welcome shade of trees and a large clearing. From here, turn right, and follow the wide track for about 100m/yds, then turn left down a narrow path (cairn- and paint-marked) through the woods. It soon comes out onto the wide track again, where you turn down left for a short while, before leaving the track again, heading right down another narrow path, which takes you into the streambed itself. Follow the rocky streambed for about 100m (easy boulder-hopping), and soon the path continues off the opposite bank, widening out and passing a water tank. Shortly after, cross the wide streambed again (cairnmarked) some 100m before a gate. Then follow a wide track undulating through the woods, but turn right just before some beehives, to recross the streambed. Soon after, you will reach an original gate ... made from a bedstead! Go through, being sure to close it after you, and walk round to cross another stream.

On coming up to a tarmac lane, turn left and follow it into the quiet little hamlet of Binibona (**5h15min**). From the square in front of the houses, turn right, and follow the narrow lane straight ahead (the lane down left goes to Moscari), for another half hour, to Caimari (**5h45min**). Here turn left, right, left, right, to descend to the main road (PM213; **6h**), where you can hail down the bus, or walk to your car.

16 A SCRAMBLE UP THE PUIG TOMIR

See map on reverse of touring map
Distance/time: 12km/7.4mi; 5h30min
Grade: strenuous climb of 600m/1970ft. Risk of falling mists; two screes to be negotiated; *possibility of vertigo* at the summit and on the second scree. *Recommended only for expert mountain walkers.*
Equipment: hiking boots, long trousers, sunhat, suncream, whistle, picnic, water, walking stick, extra clothing; anorak and woollen hat in winter
How to get there and return: 🚍 to/from Lluc (Timetable 3) or 🚂 to/from Inca (Timetable 10), where you can connect with the same bus. Alternatively, Sóller/Pollença 🚍 (Timetable 9; *note restricted service*) to the KM17.4 marker on the C710, at the entrance to the Binifaldó road (saves 25min). Or 🚗 to/from Lluc, *but note:* on weekdays you can drive to the Binifaldó gates and park there, saving 1h15min *each way.* Use the walking notes below to drive there, but be alert for the water lorries on this narrow lane.
Alternative walk: Lluc — Binifaldó — Lluc. 8km/5mi; 2h45min; easy (along wide tracks), but with an ascent of 220m/720ft. Equipment: stout shoes, sunhat, water, picnic. Access/return as main walk. Follow *Walk 15* (page 118) to the 1h30min-point, where Walk 15 descends below the main track. Keep on the main route, turning right over a kind of 'bridge' and climbing steeply to the Coll Pelat. Here go right, to circle back to Menut and your car, or go left to join the road from the Coll de Sa Bataia to Lluc. Or continue to the C710, and turn left along it for 100m/yds, then go right, back down to Lluc.

More a mountaineering adventure than a walk, this scramble is only for the sure-footed. Yet anyone can enjoy the pleasant woodland walk along the lane to the foot of Tomir. If the weather is dry, and you're really fit, off we go. The views from Tomir's peak (1103m/3618ft) make the effort well worthwhile — a magnificent panorama of hills, mountains, plains, wide bays and coastline unfolds before you — an eagle's-eye view of Mallorca!

Start the walk from Lluc, following the notes for Walk 15 (page 118) to the gates of the Binifaldó water-bottling plant (**1h15min**). *(Here the Alternative walk goes off through the wide wooden gateway on the right.)*

A sign, 'Tomir', at the right of the metal gates to the water plant, indicate the point where our intrepid route up the mountain begins. Continue along beside the fence for about five minutes, then turn up sharp right, to follow the earthen path up through the trees. It quickly becomes rocky, and before we know it, we are above the tree-line, coming up onto the bare slopes of Tomir. Soon you'll come to the first scree area, said to be the remains of a glacier; go across carefully and, a few minutes later, cross a second section of the same scree. *Only after you have crossed safely* should you turn to admire the surrounding land-

scape: Lluc's valley, the double-peaked Puig de Massanella, the Puig Roig and the Puig Major…

Now hike up the steep side of the cliff, to a small rocky pass, from where Palma is visible on a clear day. Take a breather before climbing the next scree. *Extra care is needed here:* do not attempt to climb it in dangerous conditions — just after snowfall or heavy rains, or in high winds, for instance. Further up, the going becomes easier, and the rocky route veers slightly left.

At **1h55min** you will have to clamber up a rock face — not so bad now that someone has kindly anchored a rope to the rock for us. Later, the route over the rough terrain becomes less steep; keep watching for the red waymarks and the cairns. You arrive at what appears to be the top at **2h15min**, but really you are just on the long brow of Tomir, and must keep pressing on, bearing left over rocks and rosemary scrubs until you reach the true summit at **2h40min**. *Beware of the very deep snow pit just below it!* Now you have the 'world' at your feet!

Take time to admire the breathtaking panorama on all sides before you return the same way, remembering to descend the scree with caution (**5h30min**).

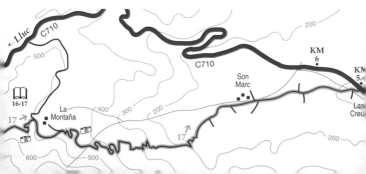

17 FROM LLUC TO POLLENÇA

Map begins on the reverse of the touring map; ends below

Distance/time: 15km/9.3mi; 4h40min from the SEFOBASA picnic area; 18km/11.2mi; 5h15min from Lluc. (From Lluc follow *Walk 15* to the house at Binifaldó (1h), then turn left below the house on a wide track, to join this walk at the 35min-point; add 35min to times below.)

Grade: easy, but fairly long. Ascent of 100m/330ft; gentle descent

Equipment: strong comfortable walking shoes or hiking boots, water, picnic, sunhat, suncream; anorak in winter

How to get there: 🚐 to Lluc (Timetable 3) or 🚋 to Inca (Timetable 10), where you can connect with the same bus. Alternatively, Sóller/Pollença 🚐 (Timetable 9; *note restricted service*) or 🚗 to the SEFO-BASA picnic area at KM16.4 on the C710

To return: 🚐 from Pollença (Timetables 6, 9; *note restricted service on Timetable 9*) back to your base or back to your parked car

Short walk: SEFOBASA picnic site — Binifaldó — SEFOBASA picnic site. 6km/3.7mi; 1h45min; easy. Equipment as main walk. Access/return: 🚗 or Sóller/Pollença 🚐 (as above) to the SEFOBASA picnic area at KM16.4 on the C710. Follow the main walk to the wide track at the 35min-point, then turn right to pass below the house of Binifaldó. Turn right again to follow the woodland lane back to Menut and the main road (C710). Here turn right back to the SEFOBASA picnic site.

A walk along the ancient Lluc/Pollença route makes a very pleasant change from the rocky mountain trails we've been following in some of the hikes. It is one of the oldest trails on the island and is known to have been a wayfarers' route since as far back as the 13th century. The wide track descends gently through beautiful mountainous landscapes, passing below the imposing north face of the Tomir mountain, and offers magnificent vistas of the craggy northeastern coastline and its wide bays.

Begin at KM16.4 on the C710, just below the SEFOBASA picnic site; alight from the bus here. Facing Lluc from the picnic site, go through the entrance gate and up the wide track on the left-hand side of the road. The track soon bends to the left and descends, to undulate through quiet woodlands. Ignore a wide but vague track off to the right some **8min** along. You'll pass by a small spring on the right (**12min**), on a bend: turn left here, passing a stone refuge. The trail becomes rockier and climbs up through the trees for another 10 minutes, then levels out (**30min**). Along here

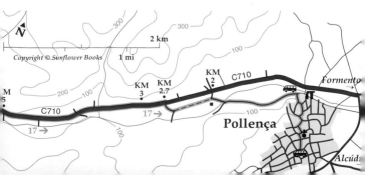

Son Marc (left) and Calvary Hill at Pollença, with the Puig de Maria in the back-ground (right)

you can see the house of Binifaldó over to the right.

At **35min** come up onto a wide stony track and turn left. *(For the Short walk turn right; this is also where you join the walk, if you come from Lluc via Binifaldó.)* Keep along the wide track, going through an access gate at the entrance to the *finca* of La Montaña some 10 minutes later. At about **1h** you will have your first magnificent view down across the pine-wooded hills and mountains towards Pollença, its port and bay, and the craggy tops of the Cavall Bernat near Cala Sant Vicenç — a beautiful vista, best enjoyed on a clear cool day. And as you continue downhill, the steep scree-covered slopes of Tomir are tremendously impressive looming up on the right at every bend. At the point where the track divides and a left turn leads past the farmhouse (**1h10min**), go right (there is usually a small cairn in the middle of the right-hand track). The track winds downhill, crosses a 'bridge' over a gushing stream, and joins another track, where you keep right again.

At just under **2h** go through a wide metal gate, and wend your way down through grassy open fields (a good place to see orchids in spring). Go through another gate about 15 minutes later, beyond which the stony trail zigzags into the valley. At about **2h40min** you'll pass a couple of beautiful houses in private grounds. Soon strange tiling comes underfoot, then tarmac. Follow this lane through farmlands and open fields, passing the lovely old stone houses of Son Marc across the stream and eventually meeting the C710 at the KM5.4 marker (**3h20min**). This junction is known as Las Creus. With luck you can catch a Sóller/Pollença bus here. If not, walk along the main road for about an hour to the KM2.7 marker, where you turn in right and then go left; a couple of minutes later, keep left along an overgrown path (just where the main track turns right). After passing a house some 10 minutes later, cross the streambed and turn left along a good road, coming into Pollença near the roman bridge. Head south through the village to the bus stop on Marques Destrull (just south of the main square.)

18 MORTITX • RAFAL D'ARIANT • SA COVA DE SES BRUIXES OVERLOOK • MORTITX

Distance/time: 8km/5mi; 5h

Grade: strenuous descents/ascents totalling about 500m/1640ft. Recommended for experienced mountain walkers; the rough and rocky terrain often makes for difficult route-finding.

Equipment: hiking boots, whistle, sunhat, long trousers, water, picnic; suncream in summer; anorak and warm clothing in winter

How to get there and return: Sóller/Pollença 🚌 (Timetable 9; *note restricted service*) to/from KM10.9 on the C710 (the Mortitx gates). Alternatively, 🚌 to Pollença (Timetable 6) and taxi to/from Mortitx (the taxi rank is near the bus stop); ask driver to return for you no later than 30 minutes before the return bus. Or by 🚗: park by the Mortitx gates (see above), without blocking the entrance.

Alternative walk: Mortitx — Coll d'es Vent — Mortitx. 8.5km/5.3mi; 4h; easy track walking. Equipment: stout shoes, water, picnic. Access/return as above. Instead of turning right just past the tennis courts at Mortitx, keep ahead on the main track, descending past some ugly farm buildings and then curving downhill to the right. At 15min go over the stile-ladder to the right of the gate, and then just keep on the main track. At 35min you pass a beautiful creek, surrounded by reeds and full of trout, and then wind up and over the hills — excellent panoramas over the Mortitx area with Tomir to the south. This part of the sierra is a protected area and an important feeding ground for black vultures; *walkers should only go in small numbers, quietly, and are requested not to leave the track.* Return the same way.

An ancient smugglers' trail leads over a wild and savage mountain landscape towards the rugged cliffs of the north coast, where pirates once risked their lives to trade in tobacco and other contraband. The scenery is almost phantasmagoric: huge boulders and wind-sculptured rocks are strewn across an uneven moonscape of ravines, valleys and jagged peaks, creating a vast and lonely wilderness, and the eerie silence, broken only by the shriek of some wild bird, lends an aura of mysticism to this unspoilt and uncivilised part of the sierra. Finally the coastal cliffs are reached, with drops of 200m/650ft to the sea. Their steep escarpments are riddled with huge caves formed by the elements, and ferocious waves beat relentlessly on the rocks below. It's a walk with a difference! And all the more exciting on a wild and windy winter's day.

Leave your transport at the Mortitx gates, and **start out** at the main entrance (or use the access gate a little lower down the road). Go over the cattle rungs at the gates, and then go through a second gate, to walk round the tennis courts. On coming to a small shed on the right, turn right through the gate (*but keep straight ahead here for the Alternative walk*). Walk down through the cherry plantations, veering left and then coming up to a locked gate

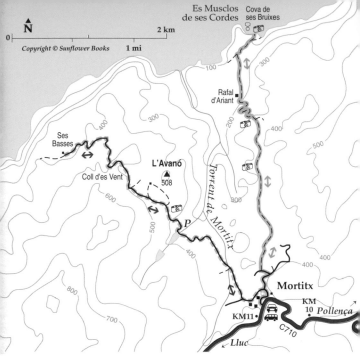

Es Musclos de ses Cordes Cova de ses Bruixes

N

2 km

0

Copyright © Sunflower Books   1 mi

100   300

Rafal
d'Ariant

200   400

300   500

Ses
Basses

400

300

L'Avanó
▲
508

Coll d'es Vent

Torrent de Mortitx

600   300

500   400

P

400

800   400   400

700

Mortitx

KM
10 *Pollença*

KM11

C710

Lluc

(**10min**). Climb the ladder placed for walkers and continue uphill to the right. The track becomes stony now and soon forks: go left. A few minutes further along, begin to look carefully for the beginning of the Camí del Rafal trail to the right of the track (marked by a large cairn). Looking carefully for the red spots, follow this narrow uneven path downhill until it levels out — now a little vague, but still waymarked. At **40min** you will come to a wall: go through the gate or over the ladder, and soon you will arrive at the point where the way goes between two huge boulders; climb up between them (on the right-hand side of the cleft, along the sloping side of the rock). The path flattens out again and it becomes a question of very careful trail-finding — be sure to follow the sporadic yellow or red spots and cairns, as the narrow rocky route winds, dips and twists across this rough and empty wilderness. At one point, the way veers left down the right-hand side of some sloping rock (about **1h**). Later it goes right, up a stony slope; here you might like to turn around for a good view of the Tomir mountain to the south, and, if you can lift your eyes from cairn-searching you might be lucky enough to see some black vultures or a red kite circling overhead.

After crossing a flattish area, go over a stone wall and then down the steepish slope on the far side of it, coming down onto the main path. *(This junction is very easily*

126

The weathered limestone terrain of Mortitx (top), and the old shepherds' hut at Rafal d'Ariant, with the cliff called 'Es Musclos de ses Cordes' in the background. The viewpoint over the Cova de ses Bruixes is at the far right-hand side of the cliff.

missed on the return; if you miss it, be sure to turn right at the faint junction a little further uphill.) Soon you will come to where the rough path descends the side of a cliff in erratic bends, from where you will have a magnificent view down over the plain of Rafal d'Ariant and the abandoned shepherds' hut below, where you arrive at about **2h**.

From here, it's only a short walk to the cliffs. Find the little path to the right of the house, veering across the flats, and then turn right through a gap in the stone wall; the earth here is a very rusty, almost volcanic colour. This path would take you down to the sea after about 20 minutes, but today we do *not* go all the way to the bottom. Go only about halfway down (as far as two huge boulders, one at the left of the path and the other slightly lower down), and veer off left here, crossing the streambed and climbing the rocky slope for a couple of minutes. When you level off, veer right across the sparse scrubs and rocks, eventually coming to a rocky platform some 100m/330ft above the sea. Take *extra care* here at the unprotected drop! To the left you can see a huge hole in the side of the cliff — the Cova de ses Bruixes (the 'Witches Cave').

Return to the shepherds' house and then retrace your steps up the cliff. Make sure you turn right at the easily-missed junction, or you'll find yourself in a maze of rock gulleys and wilderness! You're back in Mortitx in **5h**.

127

19 THE BOQUER VALLEY

Distance/time: 6km/3.7m; 2h30min

Grade: easy — gentle ascents and descents totalling 160m/525ft

Equipment: stout shoes, sunhat, suncream, water, picnic, binoculars; swimwear and towel in summer; anorak in winter

How to get there and return: 🚌 to/from Port de Pollença (Timetable 6, 9; *note restricted service on Timetable 9*) or 🚗: park on the PM221 (Formentor road), just below the Oro Playa apartments.

Winter winds, funnelled between the jagged peaks of the Cavall Bernat and the rocky mountain ridge that protects the Port of Pollença, howl fiercely through the long wide Boquer valley. And down at the lonely cove, white foaming waves beat upon the rocks… On the other hand, in summer the valley can become a merciless heat trap, with very little shade from the burning sun, and the little cove is transformed into a still and quiet 'pool', where the cormorants dive for fish in transparent blue waters.

But the Boquer valley has for decades been a favourite haunt of 'twitchers' who, in any case, avoid the winter and summer months. Late March to May, and September to October are the best months for bird-watching. Through your binoculars, amongst some of the many birds you might hope to see (depending on the season) are stone-chats, blue rock thrushes, peregrines, ravens, goldfinches, crag martins, rock sparrows, black vultures, red kites, red-legged partridges, booted eagles, serins, Eleonora's falcons, Marmora's warblers and ospreys.

Start the walk on the road from Port de Pollença to Formentor, the PM221 (signposted), and turn up left just past the Oro Playa apartments, to find the beginning of the long tree-lined avenue leading towards the Boquer Farm, which can be seen up ahead on the ridge. Go through the large gates, and walk past the front of the house (**25min**), to go through the small gate at the end of the court-yard. Then turn up right, through another gate, coming into the valley — silent and peaceful save for the bleating of goats. The track winds gently upwards, through a 'wild west' ambush scene of fallen rocks and boulders and then levels out somewhat. It passes through a drystone wall and continues on through the open valley amongst dotted palm bushes and

Above: palm bushes in a 'wild-west' landscape.
Right: this tree-shaded rise, about halfway along the valley, provides the only shade en route (Picnic 19).

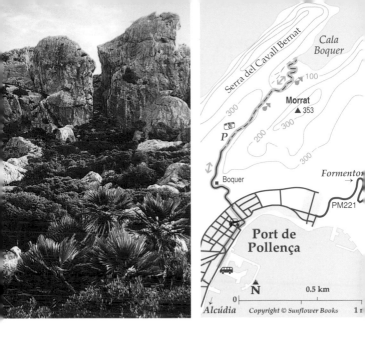

low rosemary bushes — incredible to think that you are only just around the corner from the busy port!

You'll pass one or two fresh-water springs, and at about **1h** the path narrows and descends towards the cove of Cala Boquer, which would be much more attractive if it weren't always littered with picnic remains and washed-up debris. However, if the sea is calm you might like to swim — or just sit on the rocks, enjoying the peace, looking for migratory birds or watching the sleeky black cormorants dive for fish.

Then return to the port the same way (**2h30min**).

20 ERMITA DE LA VICTORIA • PENYA ROTJA • TALAIA D'ALCUDIA • COLL BAIX • PARC DE LA VICTORIA • MAL PAS

See photographs pages 15 and 16

Distance/time: 17km/10.5 mi; 4h45min

Grade: quite strenuous climb of 450m/1475ft during the first part of the walk; easy thereafter. All good paths and tracks. *Possibility of vertigo* on the Penya Rotja. Some rock scrambling involved if you go down to Coll Baix beach.

Equipment: hiking boots or stout walking shoes, water, picnic, sunhat and suncream; anorak in winter; swimwear in summer

How to get there: 🚌 to Alcúdia (Timetables 4, 9) or Port de Pollença (Timetables 6, 9; *note restricted service on Timetable 9*). From either bus stop, taxi to the Ermita de la Victoria. Or 🚗 to the Ermita de la Victoria.

To return: taxi from Mal Pas to Alcúdia or Port de Pollença for buses, or back to your car at the *ermita*

Short walk: Ermita de la Victoria — Penya Rotja — Ermita de la Victoria. 3.5km/2.2mi; 1h25min; moderate. The ascent of 160m/520ft to the Penya Rotja path is tiring, but not difficult. This narrow path might prove vertiginous for some walkers. Equipment, access/return as main walk. Follow the main walk to the Penya Rotja viewpoint and return the same way.

Alternative walk: Ermita de la Victoria — Talaia d'Alcúdia — Coll Baix — Ses Fontanelles — Ermita de la Victoria. 9.5km/6mi; 4h30min. Grade, equipment as main walk. Access/return: 🚗 to/from the Ermita de la Victoria. This version omits the climb to Penya Rotja and allows you to walk back to your parked car at the *ermita*. Omitting the deviation to Penya Rotja, follow the main walk past the Coll Baix for about 10 minutes, then fork off right (cairn-marked) on a wide trail (really a dried-up streambed). Follow this and, about 10m/yds before it ends, go up onto the right bank of the streambed, where a narrow path begins (also cairn-marked). This vague path crosses a streambed three or four times and, after passing a fallen tree, climbs to the right up a rocky hillside. When it levels out slightly, look closely for the cairns, to dip down again to cross the streambed once more. Up the next hillside, the path becomes much easier to distinguish and eventually comes up to the Coll de ses Fontanelles, a small clearing. From here a long but gentle descent (with good views over Pollença Bay) takes us across a stream with a small dam and then to a wider dirt track. Keep ahead on this main track through an old gateway. Having ignored all turn-offs, about 1h50min from the Coll Baix you'll come to a T-junction with another wide track (in woodland). Turn up right here, and then *be sure to take the second track to the left*. It eventually narrows into an undulating path and rises steeply to the car park at the *ermita*, 2h20min from Coll Baix.

Turquoise, royal blue, pale and deep green — these are just some of the shades of the sea along the beautiful rocky coastline of the Aucanada Peninsula. Contrasting with the deep green of the pines and the sandy-coloured cliffs, this is an artist's paradise of colour. Choose a clear, cool spring day for this walk, when the air sparkles, visibility is good, and a pleasant sea breeze cools the effects of the Mallorcan sun.

The walk begins just above the car park at the church of the Ermita de la Victoria, near the picnic area (there are some public WCs just up the steps to the right of the church). Follow the wide track as it climbs quite steeply, with beautiful views down over the Bay of Pollença through the pines — this initial ascent and the fresh salty sea air will soon blow the cobwebs out of your lungs! In about **25min**, just after a sharp bend to the right, look carefully for the beginning of the narrow path to Penya Rotja, leading up left off the main track and U-turning back higher up along the cliff. *(But for the Alternative walk, keep on the track.)* This narrow path follows the contours of the Penya d'es Migdía. Just below the Penya Rotja (the 'Red Crag'), the path takes you through the 'needle eye' of an ancient watchtower and ends a couple of minutes later at a look-out point, with magnificent views of the Formentor Peninsula across the bay and down over the colourful Cap d'es Pinar (Cape of Pines) below, surrounded by many-hued

coastal waters. This is a lovely place to end the short walk with a picnic. Those not prone to vertigo can enjoy an extra frisson of excitement by climbing to the top of the Penya Rotja (355m/1165ft), where a rusty old cannon has lain silent for the past 400 years; you'll find the beginning of the rocky ascent just behind the stone bunker.

We now retrace our steps back to the main track (**1h40min**) and continue up left, rounding the Puig de Romaní and going through a wide gateway, after which the track levels off slightly. We soon come to a grassy saddle below the rocky cliff of the *talaia*. Now we begin to climb the rocky path in earnest; a slightly exposed feeling is allayed by the old wooden fencing further up, but do not lean on it! Soon after rounding the side of the mountain, we come up to the Talaia d'Alcúdia, the highest point on the route (444m/1456ft; **2h15min**). There is a splendid panorama from here: the plain stretches out below, bordered to the north by the impressive Serra de Tramuntana, and you can identify many other landscapes of our island walks — the Puig de Massanella, the Puig Tomir, the headlands of Pollença, the mountains of Artà. Below, the marshlands of S'Albufera glisten in the sun.

A few minutes down from the *talaia,* turn right (by the side of a large cairn) along a narrow rocky path which you probably didn't notice on your way up. This long descent soon leaves the *talaia* well behind and crosses the bare slopes of the Puig d'es Boc, then descends in zigzags. On one of the first bends, from a high rocky pinnacle, you have the beautiful but vertiginous view of the virgin beach of Coll Baix shown on page 16. After what seems like a thousand bends later, come to a saddle, the Coll Baix (**3h15min**). Here there is another picnic site, a drinking-water tap, and a small refuge.*

From the picnic site turn right to follow the wide track down through the trees. *(Turn right after 10 minutes for the Alternative walk.)* A long but pleasant walk follows, along a narrow tarmac lane through the woodlands of the Victoria Park. You go through the park gates at **4h15min**. Another half hour brings us to the end of the walk at the Bodega del Sol bar, at the Mal Pas crossroads (**4h45min**). From here, it's about another 2km (left), back to Alcúdia — or order a taxi from the bar and enjoy a drink while you wait.

*It takes 25 minutes to descend left to the beach. The path may still be hampered by fallen trees, and the last lap involves some clambering over large rocks. *Only swim if it is a very calm day: there is an extremely powerful undertow.* The climb back up is quite strenuous.

21 CALA ESTRETA • CALA MALSOC • TORRE D'AUBARCA • PLATJA D'ES VERGER • CALA ESTRETA

Distance/time: 8.5km/5.3mi; 3h

Grade: easy coastal path most of the way, with some walking over rocks (minimal ascents/descents)

Equipment: stout shoes, sunhat, suncream, water, picnic; towel and swimwear in summer; anorak in winter

How to get there and return: 🚌 to/from Artà (Timetable 1), then taxi from Artà to Cala Estreta and back. Phone for a taxi from a café (tel: 562202), as the taxi rank is not by the bus stop. Arrange for the taxi driver to pick you up not less than half an hour before the return bus departure. Or 🚗 to/from Cala Estreta. Leave Artà on the road to Capdepera (C715). Pass the turn-off for the prehistoric settlement of Ses Paisses after 0.3km and, 0.8km further on, turn left at the T-junction, then take the first right (just past the football ground). Follow this rough tarmac road for about 10km. Drive through an entrance, and keep left at any forks, coming down to the sea where the road curves back south. Park well to the side of the road.

Short walk: Cala Estreta — Torre d'Aubarca — Cala Estreta. 3km/2mi; 1h. Easy. No special equipment required, but be sure to take water on a hot day. Access/return by 🚗. Follow the main walk to the tower and return the same way.

The salty sea spray splashes over the bare rocks and stings your cheeks as you walk along the deserted headlands of the rugged northeastern coastline on the Artà Peninsula. Here there are several secluded sandy beaches, far enough away from civilisation to be deserted — even in summer, and the island of Menorca can be seen floating mystically on a hazy blue horizon. Yet there is an air of desolation hanging over these lonely hills — their once thickly-wooded pine slopes ravaged by multiple forest fires over the years have turned this into a bare and lifeless landscape, where only the tougher shrubs and palm bushes eke out an arid existence, and the sandy soil is held together by wild chamomile scrub. Fortunately there are still some small areas of sea-pine forest along the coast.

The walk begins on the left-hand side of the road (as you face the sea). Walk towards a wire fence that runs down to the shore (a path running parallel with the road comes in here from further uphill, should you wish to join it further

Torre d'Aubarca

up, by the side of two small palm trees). Follow the narrow rocky path round the headland, and at **10min** come to a rusty gate at the end of the fence. Go through, being careful on this cliff-edge, and follow the red waymarks around the rugged headland, amongst aromatic spiky chamomile bushes. Soon you'll see the ancient watchtower of Aubarca on the far side of the next bay. Come to beautiful Cala Malsoc at **30min**, deserted and unspoilt, its wide sandy beach edged by a forest of low sea pines. Swimming here in summer is delightful.

To continue, walk to the opposite end of the beach, near the sea, and find a sandy recess where the path up onto the next headland begins. It takes you gradually above the sea and to the watchtower (**50min**), where the large rocks of the Faralló d'Aubarca jut up out of the sea nearby. Magnificent coastal views are to be had from the tower — all along the jagged coastline towards the high cliffs and the Artà mountains.

From the tower take the wide track straight ahead of you, entering the trees. On coming to a wide shady clearing, turn right off the track, just before a sturdy old pine. You should see a cairn or two here by the side of two slender pines; go between them to descend the rather steep, stony path down onto the flatter coastal path. Now it's just a question of following the open coast. The rocky path rises and dips gently, passing the 'hidden' beach of Font Salada (the 'Salty Spring'; **1h15min**) and widens out to a track as it rounds another headland just above the sea. Pass two solitary tamarind trees, and at **1h30min** you will arrive at the beautiful long beach of Es Verger. In summer its deserted, virgin-white sands and crystal-clear blue waters are very reminiscent of the Carribean; in winter the beach is wild and invigorating. Enjoy your picnic on the beach, or a swim if you've come in warm weather, and remember to leave no litter to spoil this idyllic spot before returning to Cala Estreta along your outgoing route (**3h**).

22 CALA PI • CAP BLANC • CALA PI

Distance/time: 14km/8.7mi; 4h

Grade: easy cliff-top walking after an initial short climb up the low cliff at Cala Pí. Some danger of vertigo where the path nears the edge of the cliff just at the outset.

Equipment: strong walking shoes, water, picnic, suncream, sunhat; swimwear and towel in summer; anorak in winter

How to get there and return: 🚍 or 🚐 (see departure times page 137) to/from Cala Pí

Short walk: Cala Pí — Cala Beltrán — Cala Pí. 4km/2.5mi; 1h. Grade, equipment, access/return as above. Follow the main walk for 30min and return the same way.

This lovely coastal walk allows you to focus on the island's fauna and flora. Seagulls and cormorants, thrushes, rock lizards, perhaps herons and other migratory birds in spring or autumn, and kingfishers have all been spotted in the creek ... as well as many interesting varieties of plant life, including wild thyme and rosemary bushes, wild olive, and the occasional tamarind tree. Moreover, the pink sandstone coating the limestone on these cliffs displays wonderfully-interwoven designs where the elements have carved intricate patterns in the rock. This walk makes a complete change from walking in the mountains, and in warmer weather you can swim in one of the pretty coves.

The walk begins at the steps down to the wide creek at Cala Pí. Descend to the beach, and cross over to walk alongside the boathouses. (After torrential rains this beach can be washed away, in which case you would have to cross the water on planks.) About 50m/yds before the end of the beach, turn up right by the side of the last of the fishermen's houses and walk onto its flat roof, to find the beginning of the rough steps up the cliffs. Once at the top, leave a marker of some sort, as this point of descent is not easily seen on the return. Then turn left to follow the cliff

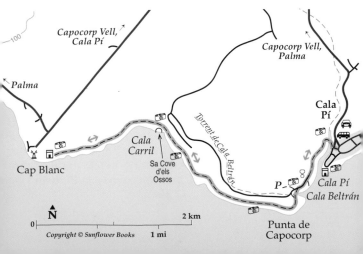

Cala Pí

path. Soon it descends a little gulley, then rises again, before going through a gap in an old stone wall. *Do* stop and turn round just beyond the wall, for the best view of beautiful Cala Pí creek, an ideal spot for photography. Then walk on, past scented shrubs, being *extremely careful* where the path skirts the edge of the cliff. Now you have a good view of the watchtower atop the cliff on the opposite side of the cove. At **20min** keep left just before a group of shady pines, and meet a wide track that rounds the cove of Cala Beltrán; end the short walk here, exploring the many criss-cross paths around the edge of this wild and pretty creek. The water in the tiny cove is usually clear and invites you to swim on a calm day, but do not attempt to swim when there is a heavy swell — the force of the waves coming in between the narrow rock walls is tremendous.

To continue the main walk, round the cove of Cala Beltrán on the wide track through the trees (there is a short-cut across marked by a cairn), and come onto the open cliffs on Capocorp Point at **30min**. Turn right to follow the rocky cliffs between rock pools, and just make your way along the different levels, enjoying the sea breeze, and watching the cormorants dive for fish. If it is a clear day and visibility is good, the rocky islands of Cabrera are easily seen on the horizon. When you come to the point where two tamarind trees stand bravely against the sea winds, by some trickling water seeping out of the rocks, you should climb onto the higher levels to continue.

At **1h20min** you might spot a red arrow painted on a large rock, but do not turn inland as it would suggest — continue along the cliff-tops, where you will soon find the easily-followed path that rounds the bay of Es Carril. It goes through one or two drystone walls, and in **2h** you reach the military boundary fence which blocks access to the watchtower just ahead. The fence is broken, and I suppose many carry on to the tower, but officially this is forbidden.

Leaving Cap Blanc, enjoy different views on the return, among them the huge Cove d'els Ossos (the 'Cave of Bones'), and many other smaller ones, at the foot of these impressive cliffs, but please remember to *take extreme care* along this high cliff-edge. You return to Cala Pí in **4h**.

TRANSPORT TIMETABLES

Timetables are given on pages 138-139 for all the transport used to get to the walks and picnics in this book. Use the alphabetical list of destinations below to find the appropriate timetable. Also shown below are some other departure times which you might find useful. **Do *not* rely solely on these timetables.** Get an up-to-date list from the tourist information office when you arrive on the island. Most timetables shown here operate in winter, and there may be more frequent departures in summer. ('Summer' timetables are usually valid from 1.5 until 30.9, but this period is flexible — it depends on the weather and how many tourists are about!) Moreover, it always pays to check the validity of timetables in advance with the transport company — no matter which timetables you use — those in this book or even the ones from the tourist office! If you are staying outside Palma, enquire at your hotel about useful local bus services in your area; ***there are many more services than those listed here***. See pages 8-9 for town plan of Palma and where to board the appropriate bus. *All departures are daily, unless otherwise coded.*

Destination	departs *from* Palma	departs *for* Palma
Alaró	08.30b, 09.00e, 13.30b, 18.00e, 19.30b	07.45b, 09.15b, 09.30e, 15.30b, 18.30e
Alcúdia	Timetables 4 and 9*	Timetables 4 and 9*
Andratx	Timetables 5 and 7	Timetables 5 and 7
Artà	Timetable 1	Timetable 1
Banyalbufar	10.00e, 13.00bc, 16.15f	08.15, 17.45e
Caimari	Timetable 3	Timetable 3
Cala d'Or	09.30, 14.45b, 19.30	07.15, 09.20b, 12.40b, 17.00
Cala Pí	07.45ab, 13.00ab, 17.00ab	09.20ab, 18.30ab
Cala Rajada	Timetable 1	Timetable 1
Cala Sant Vicenç	Timetable 9*	Timetable 9*
Ca'n Picafort (see also Timetable 9)	09.00, 13.30b, 19.00	07.00, 08.00e, 09.00b, 15.00b, 17.30e
Colònia Sant Jordi	09.30, 12.00b, 14.45b, 19.30	07.45, 13.20b, 17.40
Coves del Drac	10.00, 12.00e	14.50, 16.00b, 17.35e
Cúber Lake	Timetable 9*	Timetable 9*
Deià	Timetable 8	Timetable 8
Escorca	Timetable 9*	Timetable 9*
Estellencs	10.00e, 13.00bc, 16.15f	08.15, 17.45e
Inca	Timetables 3, 4, 6, 10	Timetables 3, 4, 6, 10
Lloseta	Timetable 10	Timetable 10
Lluc	Timetables 3 and 9*	Timetables 3 and 9*
Peguera	Timetable 5	Timetable 5
Petra	10.00e, 13.00b, 16.30b, 19.30	07.30b, 08.00e, 15.10b, 18.00
Pollença	Timetables 6 and 9*	Timetables 6 and 9*
Port d'Alcúdia	Timetables 4 and 9*	Timetables 4 and 9*
Port d'Andratx	Timetable 5	Timetable 5
Port de Pollença	Timetables 6 and 9*	Timetables 6 and 9*
Port de Sóller	Timetables 8, 9*, 12*, 13*	Timetables 8, 9*, 12*, 13*
Porto Cristo	10.00, 12.00b, 13.30b, 16.30, 17.30b, 19.30	08.10b, 09.40b, 10.25b, 14.50, 16.00b, 17.40
S'Arracó	Timetable 7*	Timetable 7*
Sa Calobra	Timetables 9* and 13*	Timetables 9* and 13*
Sant Elm	Timetable 7*	Timetable 7*
Santa Eugènia	Timetable 2	Timetable 2
Santa Maria	Timetables 6, 10	Timetables 6, 10
Sencelles	Timetable 2	Timetable 2
Sóller	Timetables 8, 9*, 11, 12*	Timetables 8, 9*, 11, 12*
Valldemossa	Timetable 8	Timetable 8

*indicates services operating outside Palma

a — in summer; b — not on Sundays or holidays; c — not on Saturdays;
d — in winter; e — only on Sundays and holidays; f — only on Saturdays

1 🚌 Palma • Manacor • Artà • Cala Rajada

	Mondays to Saturdays				Sundays/holidays
Palma	10.00	13.30	17.30	19.30	19.30
Manacor	10.50	14.20	18.20	20.20	20.20
Artà	11.30	15.00	19.00	21.00	21.00
Cala Rajada	12.00	15.30	19.30	21.30	21.30
Cala Rajada	07.45	14.30	17.10		07.45	17.10
Artà	08.15	15.00	17.40		08.15	17.40
Manacor	08.55	15.40	18.20		08.55	18.20
Palma	09.45	16.30	19.10		09.45	19.10

2 🚌 Palma • Santa Eugènia • Sencelles

	Mondays to Fridays		Saturdays	Sundays/holidays
Palma	13.30	19.00	13.30	09.00
Santa Eugènia	14.05	19.35	14.05	09.35
Sencelles	14.20	19.50	14.20	09.50
Sencelles	07.25	15.10	07.40	18.40
Santa Eugènia	07.40	15.25	07.55	18.55
Palma	08.15	16.00	08.30	19.30

3 🚌 Palma • Inca • Caimari • Lluc
(also connects with the train from Palma)

Palma	09.00e	10.00b	16.30b		Lluc	11.45b	17.00e	18.00b
Inca	09.30e	10.30b	17.00b		Caimari	12.00b	17.15e	18.15b
Caimari	09.50e	10.50b	17.20b		Inca	12.15b	17.30e	18.30b
Lluc	10.05e	11.05b	17.35b		Palma	12.45b	18.00e	19.00b

4 🚌 Palma • Inca • Alcúdia • Port d'Alcúdia

	Mondays to Saturdays(d)				Sundays/holidays(d)			
Palma	09.45	12.00c	13.30	18.00	09.45	18.00	21.00	
Inca	10.15	12.30c	14.00	18.30	10.15	18.30	21.30	
Alcúdia	10.45	13.00c	14.30	19.00	10.45	19.00	22.00	
Port	11.00	13.15c	14.45	19.15	11.00	19.15	22.15	
Port	07.45	09.15	10.15c		07.45	14.15	19.00	16.15
Alcúdia	08.00	09.30	10.30c		08.00	14.30	19.15	16.30
Inca	08.30	10.00	11.00c		08.30	15.00	19.45	17.00
Palma	09.00	10.30	11.30c		09.00	15.30	20.15	17.30

5 🚌 Palma • Peguera • Andratx • (Port d'Andratx)

Frequent departures, too numerous to list. Approximate journey times: Palma — Peguera: 40min; Peguera — Andratx: 20min; Andratx — Port: 15min. In winter buses depart Palma daily at 07.00 (08.00 Sundays/holidays) and approximately every 45 minutes thereafter until 19.30; depart Andratx 06.55 and approximately every 45 minutes thereafter until 20.00. About 5-6 buses a day go on to the Port. In summer services are more frequent. Use this service to connect with buses for Sant Elm and S'Arracó (see Timetable 7 below).

6 🚌 Palma • Santa Maria • Inca • Pollença and Port

	Mondays to Saturdays				Sundays/holidays		
Palma	10.00	13.30	17.30	19.15	10.00	16.30	20.30
Santa Maria	10.20	13.50	17.50	19.35	10.20	16.50	20.50
Inca	10.40	14.10	18.10	19.55	10.40	17.10	21.10
Pollença	11.00	14.30	18.30	20.15	11.00	17.30	21.30
Port de Pollença	11.15	14.45	18.45	20.30	11.15	17.45	21.45
Port de Pollença	07.15	09.00	14.00	17.30	08.00	14.45	18.45
Pollença	07.30	09.15	14.15	17.45	08.15	15.00	19.00
Inca	07.50	09.35	14.35	18.05	08.35	15.20	19.20
Santa Maria	08.10	09.55	14.55	18.25	08.55	15.40	19.40
Palma	08.30	10.15	15.15	18.45	09.15	16.00	20.00

7 🚌 Andratx • Sant Elm ('No 5' bus, via S'Arracó)

Andratx	08.15	14.15	16.15	18.15		Sant Elm	08.45	10.45	12.45
Sant Elm	08.40	14.40	16.40	18.40		Andratx	09.10	11.10	13.10

Codes a — e are shown in the footnote opposite

8 🚌 Palma • Valldemossa • Deià • Sóller and Port

Winter (1 October — 30 April)

Palma	07.30b	10.15	12.00b	16.15	19.30
Valldemossa	08.00b	10.45	12.30b	16.45	20.00
Deià	08.15b	11.00	12.45b	17.00	20.15
Port de Sóller**	08.45b	11.30	13.15b	17.30	20.45
Port de Sóller**	07.30	09.30b	14.30	16.00b	18.00
Deià	08.00	10.00b	15.00	16.30b	18.30
Valldemossa	08.20	10.30b	15.30	17.00b	19.00
Palma	08.50	11.00b	16.00	17.30b	19.30

Summer (1 May — 30 September)

Palma	07.30	10.15	12.00	16.15	19.30
Valldemossa	08.00	10.45	12.30	16.45	20.00
Deià	08.15	11.00	12.45	17.00	20.15
Port de Sóller	08.45	11.30	13.15	17.30	21.45
Port de Sóller	07.30	09.30	14.30	16.00	18.00
Deià	08.00	10.00	15.00	16.30	18.30
Valldemossa	08.20	10.30	15.30	17.00	19.00
Palma	08.50	11.00	16.00	17.30	19.30

9 🚌 Ca'n Picafort — Port de Sóller (or Sa Calobra)

Summer services (daily except Sundays; winter service may be very restricted)

Departures	Bus 5	Bus 7	Bus 5	Departures	Bus 5	Bus 7	Bus 5
Ca'n Picafort	09.15	09.30	15.15	Port Sóller	09.15	begins	15.30
Port Alcúdia	09.40	09.55	15.40	Sóller	09.30	at Sa Calobra,	15.45
Alcúdia	09.50	10.05	15.50	Ses Barques	09.55	departing	16.05
Port Pollença	10.00	10.15	16.00	Escorca	10.15	15.00	16.15
Cala S Viçenç	10.10	10.25	16.10	Lluc	10.30	16.30	16.30
Pollença	10.25	10.40	16.25	Pollença	11.15	17.05	17.05
Lluc	11.00	11.15	17.00	Cala S Viçenç	11.20	17.20	17.20
Escorca	11.15	goes on	17.15	Port Pollença	11.30	17.30	17.30
Ses Barques	11.35	to Sa	17.35	Alcúdia	11.40	17.40	17.40
Sóller	11.50	Calobra,	17.50	Port Alcúdia	11.50	17.50	17.50
Port Sóller	12.00	arriving 12.15	18.00	Ca'n Picafort	12.15	18.15	18.15

10 🚆 Palma • Santa Maria • Lloseta • Inca*

Departs Palma (Mon-Fri): 06.00, 07.00, 08.00, 08.40, 09.20, 10.00, 11.00, 12.00, 12.40, 13.20, 14.00, 14.40, 15.20, 16.00, 17.00, 18.00, 19.00, 20.00, 20.40, 21.20; *departs Palma (Sat, Sun/holidays):* every hour on the hour from 06.00-21.00
Departs Inca (Mon-Fri): 07.00, 08.00, 08.40, 09.20, 10.00, 11.00, 12.00, 12.40, 13.20, 14.00, 14.40, 15.20, 16.00, 17.00, 18.00, 19.00, 20.00, 20.40, 21.20; 22.00; *departs Inca (Sat, Sun/holidays):* every hour on the hour from 06.00-21.00
*Stops at Santa Maria 19min from Palma and at Lloseta 32min from Palma; stops at Lloseta 4min from Inca and at Santa Maria 18min from Inca

11 🚆 Palma • Sóller

Palma	08.00	10.40	13.00	15.15	19.45d	20.05a
Sóller	09.00	11.45	14.00	16.15	20.45d	21.00a
Sóller	06.45	09.15	11.50	14.10	18.20d	19.00a
Palma	07.45	10.15	12.50	15.10	19.20d	20.00a

12 🚌 Sóller • Port de Sóller • Sóller

Departs Sóller: 05.55, 07.00, 08.00, 09.00, 10.00, 11.00, 11.30, 12.00, 12.30, 13.00, 14.00, 15.00, 16.00, 16.30, 17.00, 17.30, 17.55, 19.00, 20.00, 20.45
Departs Port: 06.20, 07.30, 08.25, 09.30, 10.30, 11.30, 12.00, 12.30, 13.00, 13.25, 14.30, 15.30, 16.30, 17.00, 17.30, 17.55, 18.30, 19.30, 20.20, 21.10

13 ⛴ Port de Sóller • Sa Calobra

Daily (depending on the weather): telephone 633109 for information

Departs				Arrives			
Port de Sóller	10.30	11.30	15.00	Sa Calobra	11.20	12.20	15.50
Sa Calobra	14.00	15.00	16.45	Port de Sóller	14.50	15.50	17.35

**bus calls at Sóller (Plaça América) 10 minutes before the Port en route *from* Palma, calls at Sóller 5-10 minutes after the Port en route *to* Palma; a — in summer; b — not on Sundays or holidays; c — not on Saturdays; d — in winter; e — only on Sundays and holidays

 Index

Geographical names comprise the only entries in this index; for non-geographical subjects, see Contents, page 3. A page number in *italic type* indicates a map; **bold type** refers to a photograph or drawing. Both of these may be in addition to a text reference on the same page. 'TM' refers to the walking map on the reverse of the touring map. Pronunciation hints follow all place names.

GLOSSARY

(M) Mallorquín; (S) Spanish;

atalaya (S) — *see* talaia
avenc (M) — crater, deep pit
baix (M), *bajo* (S) — low
barranc (M), *barranco* (S) — ravine
*caça a coll (M) — thrush-netting
caçador (M) — hunter
camí (M), *camino* (S) — road, way
ca'n (M) — 'case d'en' ('house of')
canaleta (S) — *see* síquia
carrer (M), *calle* (S) — street
*casa de neu (M), *casa de nieve* (S) — snow pit
coll (M), *collado* (S) — saddle
*coll de caçar (M) — place for thrush-netting (literally, 'hunting at the saddle')
coma (M) — valley floor
comedero (S) — feeding ground
cordillera (S) — mountain range
coto privado de caza (S) — private hunting ground; *see also* vedat
cova, cove (M), *cueva* (S) — cave
dalt (M), *alto* (S) — high
embalse (S) — reservoir
ermita (M, S) — hermitage
estret (M) — narrow pass
finca (S) — farm
font (M), *fuente* (S) — spring
fronton (M) — pelota court

*forn de calç (M), *horno de cal* (S) — lime oven
mij (M), *medio* (S) — middle
mola (M) — table mountain
morro (M, S) — cliff-top
pas (M) — mountain pass
passeig (M), *paseo* (S) — walk or walkway
penya (M), *pena* (S) — cliff
pla (M), *planicie* (S) — plain
platja (M), *playa* (S) — beach
pou (M), *pozo* (S) — well
puig (M), *pico* (S) — mountain
*santuari (M) — hermitage, monastery
senda (S) — footpath, trail
serra (M), *sierra* (S) — mountain range
*síquia (M), *canaleta* (S) — irrigation channel, watercourse
*sitja (M) — fireplace used in the charcoal industry
son (M) — 'estate of'
*talaia (M), *atalaya* (S) — ancient watchtower
talaiot (M) — prehistoric stone structure
torrent (M), *torrente* (S) — stream (Mallorca has no rivers)
vedat (M) — private hunting ground
vell (M), *viejo* (S) — old

*see pages 58-63 for more details

143

RIGHTS OF WAY AND THE ADIM

If, when you are out walking, you come across a closed-off route that you know was previously open to walkers, you can go to the town hall of that municipality and ask for information. Some routes are closed without the town hall being properly informed by the landowners, and may still be publicly accessible.

The ADIM (Association for the Defense of Itineraries in Mallorca) was formed in 1996 to try to protect walkers' rights of way. Their aims are described below. If you would like to become an associate member, write to them at: ADIM, Carrer Pau 5, Palma, and ask them to send you a membership form and information about the fee for joining. They would certainly be interested in hearing from you, if you encounter any problems on the walks described in this book: write to them direct, or write to me at: Carrer de Ses Monges, 9 — 1°, Santa Eugenia.

❖

The Association for the Defense of Itineraries in Mallorca is an entity dedicated to the conservation, promotion and defense of hiking itineraries in Mallorca, and its main objectives are:

— To study, investigate and promote the cultural patrimony of the hiking routes of Mallorca, especially in the mountainous regions.

— To defend the cultural patrimony of our mountains and in particular the hiking itineraries, as well as access to these for everyone.

— Promote access to mountains with respect for the inhabitants therein and for the environment.

❖

The ADIM came into being due to the ever-increasing attempts to restrict or even prohibit access to the mountain hiking itineraries.

From the ADIM we wish to coordinate the efforts of all those who are affected by these restrictions and prohibitions, such as hikers, or those who simply wish to visit and enjoy the beauty of our mountains.

The ADIM wishes to collect all kinds of information about these itineraries, especially up in the Sierra, and especially of those routes which are becoming, or have become, problematic, and at the same time be able to inform hikers and others of their rights, and any possible action that may be taken.

To carry out these objectives, to be able to put pressure on the various authorities, and to be able to further our cause, we need your help. That's why we're asking you to become an associate of the ADIM.

To deal with any of the aforesaid, and to try to solve these problems, common to us all, we can be found at No 5 Carrer Pau (just off the Borne) every Thursday evening from 19.00h (7pm) to 20.00h (8pm). We can also be reached by telephone at the following number: 246019.